Business Basics

A Microbusiness Startup Guide

Gerard Dodd

with illustrations by Tim Sample

OASIS PRESS BOOKS & SOFTWARE
Celebrating 25 Years

The Oasis Press®
Central Point, OR

Published by The Oasis Press®

Business **Basics**: A Microbusiness Startup Guide
© 1998, by Gerard Dodd, with illustrations by Tim Sample

Please direct any comments, questions, or suggestions regarding this book to The Oasis Press® at the following address:

    PSI Research
    The Oasis Press® Editorial Dept.
    P.O. Box 3727
    Central Point, Oregon 97502

    info@psi-research.com   email
    (541) 479-9464
    (800) 228-2275

The Oasis Press® is a registered trademark of Publishing Services, Inc., an Oregon corporation doing business as PSI Research.

Library of Congress Cataloging-in-Publication Data
Dodd, Gerard R.
   Business basics : a microbusiness startup guide / by Gerard Dodd '
  with illustrations by Tim Sample.
       p.   cm. -- (PSI successful business library)
  Includes index.
   ISBN 1-55571-430-7 (pbk.)
   1. New business entreprises--Management. 2. Small business-
-Management. 3. Entrepreneurship. 4. Self-employed. I. Title.
II. Series.
HD62.5.D626   1998
658.02'2--dc21   9752777
                                                   CIP

Printed and bound in the United States of America
   Printed on recycled paper when available.

Acknowledgments
& Dedication

To the thousands of micro businesspeople throughout Main who enthusiastically shared their wisdom and experiences with me in workshops and consultations.

To everyone directly or indirectly involved with The Maine Idea who made the first edition of *Management Workbooks for Self-employed People* possible.

To micro businesspeople throughout Maine and the rest of the country. May your business flourish and may you stay on the cutting edge of socio-economic change.

Table of Contents

DOG WAGGING TAIL

THIS

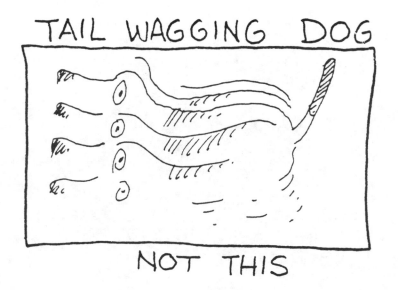

TAIL WAGGING DOG

NOT THIS

MANAGE YOUR BUSINESS!

Introduction

The concept of a "micro" or "mini" business is used to distinguish small time operators (home-based businesses, "mom and pop" shops, crafts people, service people, etc.) from larger "small businesses. Micro businesses are now recognized as a major component of the U.S. economy.

I find that micro business people, in general, take pride in the quality of their products and services, but are hampered by their limited management skills. The material presented here is based on the observations and expressed needs of micro business people. It was acquired largely through management workshops and personal conversations with outstanding entrepreneurs.

In this book, you will find plenty of helpful hints but no magic formulas--running a business is hard work. My goal is to improve your understanding of basic management practices, thereby helping you make that aspect of your business more agreeable and rewarding. This concisely presented information points you in the right direction and gets you asking the right questions.

Although my experience includes many years of running micro businesses, I have never considered myself a business "expert" or a high-powered entrepreneur. I am a good listener who has the ability to see business basics from a fresh perspective. Tim Sample's drawings certainly typify the friendly, less-threatening approach to management that I advocate. Through his "typical" micro business family--Helen, Joe and Ralph (the dog)-- Time makes complex concepts more meaningful and accessible.

WHO CAN BENEFIT FROM THIS BOOK?

Let's face it, some people are just naturally gifted entrepreneurs. They combine energy and drive with an intuitive knack for doing the right thing at the right time. If you are one of these people, you may not need this book.

Other folks, more like myself, are hard-working and conscientious but not especially blessed with great business acumen. They are good at what they do, but they would just as soon not put lots of energy into managing or marketing or putting together business plans or wheeling and dealing. These are the people who can most benefit from *Business Basics*.

Finally, there are those who view being in business for themselves as a way out of something else. Their business ideas are sketchy and unclear, and they are not particularly service-oriented. These folks may not be cut out for small business and are advised to carefully evaluate their interests and entrepreneurial abilities before going any further.

HOW THIS BOOK IS STRUCTURED AND HOW TO USE IT

There are six sections. Here's an overview:

Section One: Management and Entrepreneurship gives you some tools for better defining your business ideas and putting them into a wider context. It includes the crucial concept of developing a "complete idea."

Section Two: Basic Marketing helps you appraise and target your market. It guides you step-by-step through the process of developing a promotional strategy.

Section Three: Basic Finances shows you how to manage the finances using simple bookkeeping procedures that work for you. It introduces you to the vital concept of cash flow management.

Section Four: Capital and the Business Plan prepares you for going to the bank. It tells you what to expect and shows you how to increase the likelihood of success by creating the right impression.

Section Five: Time and Personnel guides you through the more challenging waters of managing human resources. It outlines hiring considerations and helps you get set up right from the start.

Section Six: Activity Planning provides the planning tools you need to pull everything together into a sensible, doable overall plan. Having such a plan heightens your chances of success.

Some people use the book as a guide to doing an overall business review once or twice a year. Others use it for specific problem-solving or to meet special needs. Someone in the early stages of business may dedicate more time and effort to marketing, while someone who is more established focuses on time and personnel issues. Still others use the book only as a reference manual when questions come up.

Business Basics will take some of the mystery out of small business management for you. In doing so, I hope it motivates you to really move into the driver's seat of your business so that you can experience the deep sense of satisfaction and accomplishment that comes from a well-run enterprise.

Gerry Dodd

February, 1998

A MICRO BUSINESS is the smallest economic venture—usually owner-operated with few employees and less than $200,000 annual sales. Most craftspeople, service people, small farmers, "mom and pop" shops, cooperatives, and alternative businesses are micro businesses.

The terms "self-employed person," "small time operator," and "micro (or mini) businessperson" are used interchangeably in this book.

Section One:

Management & Entrepreneurship

YOU'RE THE "EXPERT" IN YOUR BUSINESS

Every business is different. Only you can decide which direction you want your business to take. You decide how to deal with weaknesses or problems and how to capitalize on advantages and assets.

When was the last time you really analyzed all the different aspects of your business? That long ago?

By now, you've probably discovered a few of the hard truths about being in business for yourself — there are no 40 hour weeks, regular paychecks or paid vacations. There **are** certain rewards — being your own boss, offering a quality product, financial independence. Despite frustration and long hours, most micro businesspeople wouldn't have it any other way!

Here's another point: To be successful you've got to be a jack-of-all-trades — owner, manager, chief mechanic and salesperson all in one. Just turning out good work isn't enough. You have to organize, finance, package and sell it. No matter if you're a carpenter, a welder or a drugstore owner, you have to be a manager as well.

Which brings up another point: What is an entrepreneur anyway? Is there a difference between an entrepreneur and a manager?

It's time to go back to square one — to review where you are in your business and where you're going. Are your business ideas complete enough to attract the success you deserve?

By looking at all sides of the question, we **can** come up with fresh ideas

EXAMINING "WHERE YOU'RE AT" WILL HELP YOU DECIDE WHERE TO GO

IDEA BLOCKS like this are for jotting down changes you want to make and new things you want to try out in your business. Careful use of the idea blocks will help you organize your ideas into a coherent plan later on.

One-Page Management Appraisal

DOES YOUR BUSINESS HAVE AND USE...	NOW		6 MONTHS LATER	
	Yes	No	Yes	No
A BASIC PLAN OF ACTION?	☐	☐	☐	☐
...Written down?	☐	☐	☐	☐
...Including long-term directions?	☐	☐	☐	☐
...With specific objectives for annual improvement?	☐	☐	☐	☐
AN OVERALL MARKETING STRATEGY?	☐	☐	☐	☐
...Clear notion of customer preferences?	☐	☐	☐	☐
...Customer profile and competition analysis?	☐	☐	☐	☐
...A specific advertising and promotional plan?	☐	☐	☐	☐
AN EFFICIENT OPERATIONS SYSTEM?	☐	☐	☐	☐
...Organized internal systems for work planning & control?	☐	☐	☐	☐
...Efficient daily time management skills?	☐	☐	☐	☐
...An organizational structure outlining areas of responsibility?	☐	☐	☐	☐
ADEQUATE FINANCIAL CONTROL?	☐	☐	☐	☐
...Up-to-date recordkeeping used both for taxes & management?	☐	☐	☐	☐
...Cash flow projection and monthly analysis?	☐	☐	☐	☐
...Monthly and quarterly financial statements?	☐	☐	☐	☐
...Credit policy and diligent collection system?	☐	☐	☐	☐
ACCESS TO CREDIT?	☐	☐	☐	☐
...Productive banking relationships?	☐	☐	☐	☐
...Adequate supplier credit?	☐	☐	☐	☐
...Sufficient working capital?	☐	☐	☐	☐
MOTIVATED EMPLOYEES?	☐	☐	☐	☐
...Efficient personnel without chronic problems?	☐	☐	☐	☐
...Written job descriptions?	☐	☐	☐	☐
...Periodic performance evaluations?	☐	☐	☐	☐
...Clear, honest communications?	☐	☐	☐	☐
ENOUGH OUTSIDE ASSISTANCE?	☐	☐	☐	☐
...A business advisor or management service?	☐	☐	☐	☐
...An accountant used for more than just taxes?	☐	☐	☐	☐
RATING OF OVERALL SITUATION: Using a scale of very good (5), good (4), average (3), poor (2) and very poor (1), rate your performance!	☐		☐	

The entrepreneur is willing to work hard, gets along well with others, has good communication skills, knows how to organize, takes pride in what s/he does, maintains good interpersonal relations, is a self-starter, welcomes responsibility, is willing and able to make decisions.

The micro entrepreneurs we deal with have definite opinions. They think a successful micro business needs:

- An owner/manager with the right personal qualities — hard-working, good with customers, honest, self-confident, self-motivated, tenacious.
- A high quality product or service to build a reputation.
- Adequate managerial, administrative, and financial skills.
- A solid financial footing based on equity, access to credit, and sufficient working capital.

Carefully study the risk and the personal commitments involved in business — long hours, hard work, self-motivation and confidence in your abilities, honesty and fairness in working with others. If you're going to work with a partner, pick someone who is not a mirror image of yourself. Someone with different talents and skills will be much more valuable.

Should I Be in Business?

RATE YOURSELF!

	Never	Almost never	Sometimes	Most of the time	All of the time
Am I a self starter?					
Am I friendly and outgoing?					
Can I take responsibility?					
Am I organized?					
Am I a decision maker?					
Am I a leader?					
Do people trust me?					
Do I have determination?					
Do I consider other people's opinions?					

Entrepreneurs work hard at a wide variety of things. A successful entrepreneur will answer "all" or "most of the time" to most of these questions.

ARE YOU AN ENTREPRENEUR, A MANAGER OR NEITHER?

- **Entrepreneur** — an individual who invests money, energy and time in a business with the hope of making a profit; a person who organizes, operates and assumes the risk for business ventures.

- **Manager** — a person who handles or controls something; directs or administers the affairs of a business.

The Five Ingredients
of a Successful Business

- A qualified entrepreneur

- A potential business opportunity

- A solid and detailed plan

- Sufficient capital

- Luck

Taken from: *The Small Business Handbook* by Irving Burstiner

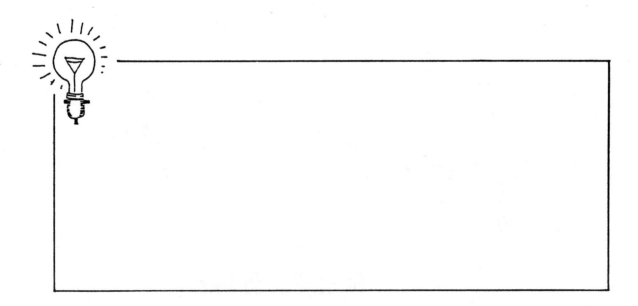

What Business Is This?

Businesses are always changing. What you started out doing years ago may be completely different today. Your motivation and personal goals change over time, and this could alter the way you operate. If you are not happy with the way things are going, make changes! You're the boss and it's your job to manage the business, rather than allowing it to manage you. Prepare a **brief** description of your business. How would you describe it to someone who knows nothing about it?

_____

_____

_____

_____

_____

_____

_____

_____

_____

_____

_____

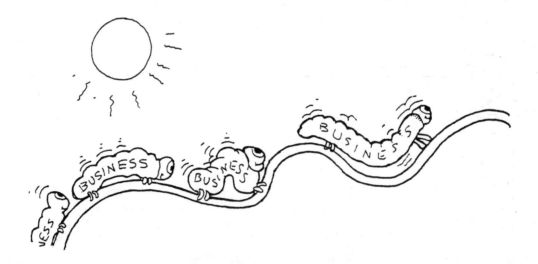

BUSINESSES ARE...

Why Am I in Business?

Take a few minutes to think about your reasons for being in business and your **major** goals. What are your personal reasons for being in business (e.g. "be my own boss," "make a million," "make a decent living"). How far along are you? What do you hope to achieve in the next two, five, or ten years? Writing your answers to these questions may tell you something about the way you approach your business.

_____

_____

_____

_____

_____

_____

_____

_____

_____

_____

_____

_____

...ALWAYS CHANGING

What Stage of Business Am I In?

PRE-STARTUP: You're thinking of going into business for yourself. Talk it over thoroughly with family, friends, potential suppliers, customers, banks, etc. Analyze your strengths and weaknesses. Take the time now, **while you can** to do research and test the market.

        TIME LINE:_____

DEVELOPMENT STAGE: You've committed yourself to it! Be careful! This is when many new businesses fail. Things usually take longer than you expect and the market response may be slower than anticipated. It takes time to build a reputation. **Start managing** by setting goals and checking performance against them.

        TIME LINE:_____

GROWTH STAGE: Until now, you've probably done most of the work yourself. The market has responded favorably and expansion is a real possibility. Avoid rapid growth for its own sake. Instead, plan carefully to increase profits. Expand in areas where you have experience or access to reliable help. Learn to delegate responsibility.

        TIME LINE:_____

COMFORT STAGE: You've put together a stable business. Your annual growth may have slowed down, but you're now deriving more benefits from the business. You're satisfied with the results. Don't become over-confident or take things for granted. Anticipate the future and possible changes which could occur.

        TIME LINE:_____

TURNAROUND STAGE: Somehow you've gotten into trouble. You're losing money; the competition is moving in and there's little or no working capital. How can you get out of this mess? Cut out **anything** non-productive — people, products, services, etc. Manage for cash. Swallow your pride and learn from your mistakes.

        TIME LINE:_____

        (Hopefully, never!)

THE KEY TO AN EFFICIENT OPERATION

Self-employed people are generally more familiar with organization and direction than with planning and control. Many small companies are so diversified that the owners lose the overall sense of where the business is going. It takes planning to pull together the loose ends.

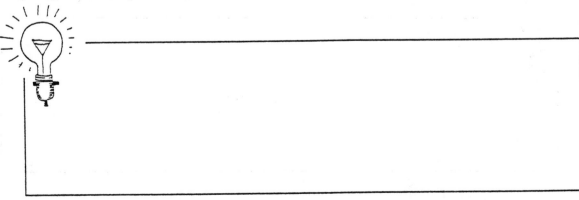

Management Involves. . .

- **PLANNING** — setting goals and deciding what's to be done. Choose practical goals that are within the scope of your resources.

- **ORGANIZING** — putting plans into action — matching people and resources with tasks. It's the "how to" of getting the job done!

- **DIRECTING** — guiding the activities you've chosen and motivating people to work more productively.

- **CONTROLLING** — measuring your level of achievement.

Excuses for not planning could fill a book. Some are valid; others are **just** excuses. If you want your company to grow and prosper, you must anticipate conditions, not just react to them. Planning could make the difference between a stable concern and one that is in trouble.

Planning helps to clarify your thoughts and identify strengths to build on. It helps you organize yourself and measure the results of your efforts.

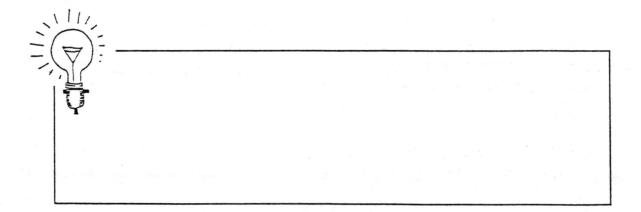

DISCOVER WHAT YOU REALLY WANT TO DO!

Thinking about goals is quite different from writing them down. Unwritten goals often remain vague or utopian dreams. Writing them down makes them more concrete and specific and helps you get below the surface of the old clichés you've been telling yourself for years.

The Planning Process

1. CONDUCT A BUSINESS REVIEW

2. COMPILE IDEAS & SET GOALS

3. PUT TOGETHER YEARLY PLAN

4. BREAK DOWN INTO MONTHS

5. EVALUATE ACHIEVEMENTS

6. REPROJECT PLANS

The Complete Idea

In *Honest Business* (Random House, 1981), Michael Phillips and Salli Rasberry discuss the "Complete Idea" concept and its relevance to the small operator:

> When you are starting a business with a new idea, work the idea out entirely, examine all its ramifications and nuances, keep developing it until you are certain of its validity and then execute it completely. The integrity of the whole will show through and your vision will be constantly supported by your customers as well as your imitators.

An example of a complete idea is the sheep farmer who, when faced with a highly seasonal meat market, decides not only to sell fleeces but to spin wool and make finished products from the spun wool. This decision alters the nature of the farmer's market and business. It complements the central business activity (raising sheep) while providing work during slack times and opening new marketing options.

It's especially important to have a clear idea of your business directions — your goals, expectations and limitations. Do your business ideas fit together in a logical way or are they scattered and inconsistent? Think about the central activities of your business. Why are you involved in this particular business? What do you hope to get out of it in the short, medium and long term? Then consider the image you and your business actually present. Are any changes needed?

Overall Goals and Directions

CURRENT SITUATION
The business size and structure
My actual customers and what I offer them
The scope of my marketing and how people perceive me
The status of my production or service delivery
My financial needs and limitations
Miscellaneous

It takes patience and careful thought to perfect a complete idea. Consider the whole picture — the overall concept behind your business. Look at your goals and consider where you want your operation to go over the short, medium and long term. How do your different ideas fit together? What's unique about your business?

Consider the strengths and weaknesses of your operation in an organized way. Set practical goals and don't water down your ideas or just accept the conventional solutions.

QUESTIONS TO ANSWER

- What do I hope to achieve?
- How big do I want to get?
- Do I have any special limitations?
- What customer needs am I targeting?
- What image do I want to project to the public?
- What are the economic realities?

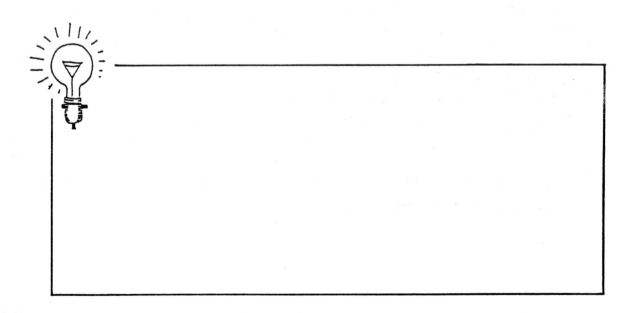

The Complete Idea — Business Goals

CONSIDERATIONS	ONE YEAR GOALS
SIZE & STRUCTURE OF BUSINESS Consider gross income, take-home pay, legal structure, workforce & principal collaborators, organizational structure, special goals or limitations...	
THE MAIN IDEA(S) Consider type of production, major products, and/or services, uniqueness, customer needs targeted, complimentarity or diversity or seasonality of products...	
PUBLIC IMAGE & MARKET Consider name, logo, location, principal (targeted) customers, geographic coverage, promotional & advertising strategy, reputation & position in the community...	
PRODUCTION & SERVICE Consider production volume, organization & workflow, equipment & facilities, suppliers, inventory, new methods or techniques...	
MANAGEMENT & FINANCE Consider internal systems & recordkeeping, working capital & credit needs, time & personnel management, activity planning...	
MISCELLANEOUS & OBSERVATIONS	

ONCE YOU'VE DEFINED OVERALL GOALS, IT'S

Business Name: _____

Period Covered: _____ to _____

THREE YEAR GOALS	FIVE YEAR GOALS

EASIER TO DEVELOP YEARLY & MONTHLY PLANS!

Daily Action List

DAY _____ DATE _____

THINGS TO DO TODAY	✔

APPOINTMENTS

TIME	PERSON	COMPANY	LOCATION

PHONE CALLS

PERSON/COMPANY	PHONE NUMBER	

Begin Planning Today

Most people who get things done and pack lots of varied activities into a day plan their days in advance by making a Daily Action or "To Do" List. This is a prioritized listing of tasks and activities (much more than a bunch of paper scraps stapled together). The list focuses on high priority tasks which could otherwise be overlooked or forgotten. Once complete, it is kept in a visible place and serves as a guide to action throughout the day.

Time management experts say that every minute spent planning can save you 20 minutes later in the day. This is because planning helps you stay focused on high priority tasks so that time isn't wasted on "urgent trivialities." Instead, focus on activities which produce the greatest benefit.

Beginning today, make a commitment to spend at least 15 minutes a day planning. Find a way to do this *in solitude and without interruptions* either the last thing at night or first thing in the morning. First, write down all non-routine things that need to be done that day. Then, assign priorities.

> **"A" = vital**
> **"B" = important**
> **"C" = some importance**

"A" priorities must be done today; "B"s can be postponed until tomorrow; and "C"s can be delayed indefinitely. Then, further prioritize into A-1, A-2, A-3, B-1, B-2, etc.

During the day, constantly refer back to your list. Any time you have a few minutes, spend them working on top priority tasks. As you complete each task, check it off and feel the satisfaction of taking charge of your business and your life.

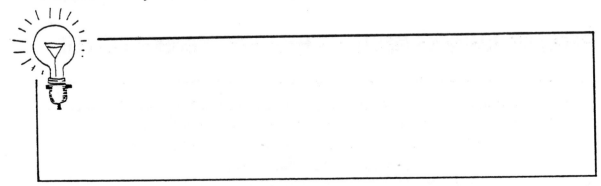

REGULAR BUSINESS MEETINGS HELP YOU MANAGE BETTER

It's only within a total framework that good time planning is possible.
A written Goals Statement helps you discover what you really
want to do, motivates you to do it and gives meaning to the
way you spend your time.

Topics for Business Meetings

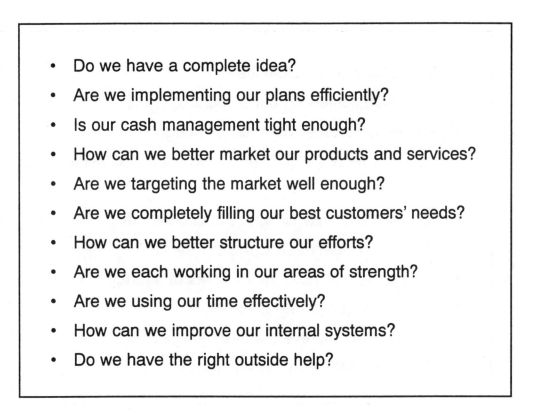

- Do we have a complete idea?

- Are we implementing our plans efficiently?

- Is our cash management tight enough?

- How can we better market our products and services?

- Are we targeting the market well enough?

- Are we completely filling our best customers' needs?

- How can we better structure our efforts?

- Are we each working in our areas of strength?

- Are we using our time effectively?

- How can we improve our internal systems?

- Do we have the right outside help?

Even though you think you're too busy to plan, you always come out ahead by planning anyway. One minute of planning saves 20 minutes of doing. Find time to do what you want to do. Think in terms of making time through careful scheduling. Don't end up dealing with *problems* instead of *opportunities.*

Topics for Business Meetings

- Do we have a complete idea?
- Are we implementing our plans efficiently?
- Is our cash management tight enough?
- How can we better market our products and services?
- Are we targeting the market well enough?
- Are we completely filling our best customers' needs?
- How can we better structure our efforts?
- Are we each working in our areas of strength?
- Are we using our time effectively?
- How can we improve our internal systems?
- Do we have the right outside help?

Even though you think you're too busy to plan, you always come out ahead by planning anyway. One minute of planning saves 20 minutes of doing. Find time to do what you want to do. Think in terms of making time through careful scheduling. Don't end up dealing with *problems* instead of *opportunities*.

Section Two:

Basic Marketing

MARKETING IS
MOVING GOODS FROM PRODUCER TO CONSUMER

OR SATISFYING CUSTOMER NEEDS AT A PROFIT!

Marketing is more than "pushing a product"; it is satisfying real customer needs to insure repeat sales. A primary objective of marketing is to develop a large pool of satisfied customers who will not only return to buy, but will also spread the word about your business because they trust your products and appreciate your personal attention.

Effective marketing is mostly a question of satisfying customer needs — at a profit. It's also the ability to use limited resources **wisely.** Since you can't be all things to all people, you have to "target your market" to those who need you most.

Too many "gut feelings" about the market may lead to serious trouble. Research and hard thinking count! Develop a customer profile to figure out what kinds of people use your business or service. Get customer reactions to prices, quality, dependability, convenience and advertising. By analyzing these things, you can pinpoint problem areas and determine more profitable ways of spending your time.

It's also important to identify consistent business patterns and seasonal trends. Try stabilizing sales with discounts during slow periods, special package sales before and after peak periods, increased personal attention at off-times, gift coupons and increased promotion.

Steps to Effective Marketing

STEP I:

DETERMINE YOUR CUSTOMERS' NEEDS

Get to know your customers. Talk with them about how your products and services fill their needs.

STEP II:

ANALYZE YOUR COMPETITIVE ADVANTAGES

By studying the competition, you learn about yourself!

STEP III:

TARGET YOUR MARKET

Focus your energy and resources on a certain income level, special interest group or geographic area.

STEP IV:

USE YOUR MARKETING MIX TO SATISFY CUSTOMER NEEDS

Each business satisfies customer needs with its own unique marketing mix — a combination of products and/or services, prices, distribution system and promotional strategy.

Step I:

Determine Your Customers' Needs

Ask your customers what they want to see in your store; talk to them informally or ask them to fill out a simple questionnaire in return for a special discount or small gift. This kind of direct feedback is invaluable in planning your marketing strategy.

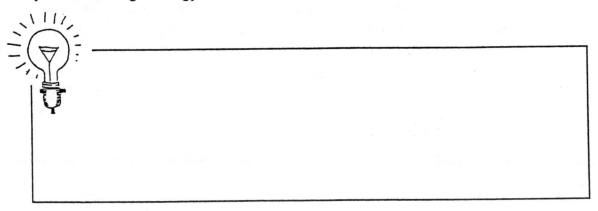

ASK YOURSELF.....

WHO are my customers? (Teenagers? Retired people? People with lots of leisure time? People with special interests?

_____

_____

_____

_____

_____

WHERE do they live? (Country? City? Suburbia? Nearby? Out-of-state?)

_____

_____

_____

_____

WHY do they use me instead of the competition? (Personalized service? Prices? Quality? Store hours? Availability of merchandise?

_____

_____

_____

_____

_____

WHEN do they come to me? (Daily? Once in a while? At unusual times?)

_____

_____

_____

_____

WHAT particular services or products are they looking for? (What are my best-selling items?)

_____

_____

_____

_____

_____

Step II:

Analyze Your Competitive Advantages

QUALITY, PRICES, GUARANTEES...
WHERE'S YOUR NICHE IN THE MARKETPLACE?

The time to analyze the competition is **all the time!** Be sure of your market position by knowing what your competitors are doing — by being informed of their products, prices and services. Talk to them!

Competitor Checklist

Who are my major competitors? What are their strengths and weaknesses? What does this tell me about my business and my marketing strategy?

	Competitor Name			Competitor Name			Competitor Name			My situation:		
	Better	Equal	Worse	Better	Equal	Worse	Better	Equal	Worse	Good	Average	Poor
Prices												
Quality												
Product Selection												
Customer Attention												
Service/Repairs												
Reliability												
Expert Advice												
Guarantees												
Customer Credit												
Credit Cards												
Location												
Store Hours												
Store Appearance												
Advertising												

Compare your prices, quality, service, reliability and customer attention. Expect to be strong in some areas, weak in others. You can't be tops in everything! If your prices and quality are superb, your service may be lacking. Carefully analyze the differences. How can you use your strengths to compensate for your weaknesses?

Step III:
<u>Target Your Market</u>

Because of your limited resources, you can't be all things to all people. Therefore, it's a question of focusing your time, energy and financial resources on those who will most benefit from your business while providing you with a fair return.

APPROACHES...

- Focus on a particular geographic area (perhaps within a 25-mile radius of your shop).

  _____

  _____

  _____

  _____

  _____

- Focus on your best-selling product or service. (If you have a winner, promote it!)

  _____

  _____

  _____

  _____

- Focus on those who are most likely to patronize your business. (If you sell farm equipment — farmers. If you sell blue jeans — teenagers.)

  _____

  _____

  _____

  _____

Once you've targeted your market and developed a "customer profile," you'll be in a better position to decide on marketing strategies and techniques. Think of ways of better reaching your targeted customers!

The 80/20 Rule of Thumb

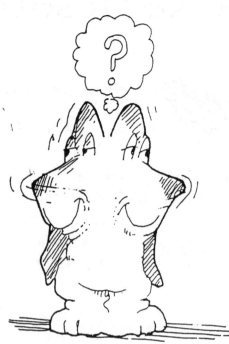

80% of your PROFITS come from...
20% of your CUSTOMERS!

80% of your SALES come from...
20% of your NORMAL PRODUCT LINE!

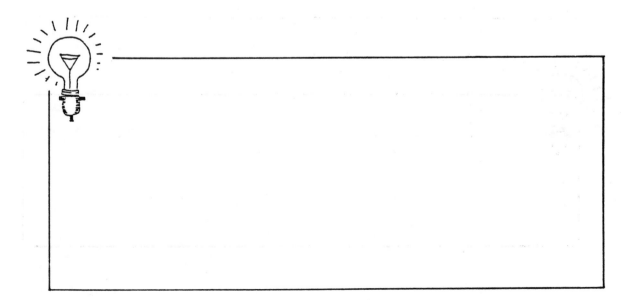

Who Are My Best Customers?

**80% of your profits come from
20% of your customers!**

Think it over! Who are the important 20%? Where do they come from?
Consider their ages, occupations, incomes, education, buying habits,
leisure activities, etc. Can you think of better ways to reach them?
Answering these questions will help you set criteria for advertising,
penetrating the market, location and many other decisions.

_____

_____

_____

_____

_____

_____

_____

_____

_____

_____

_____

_____

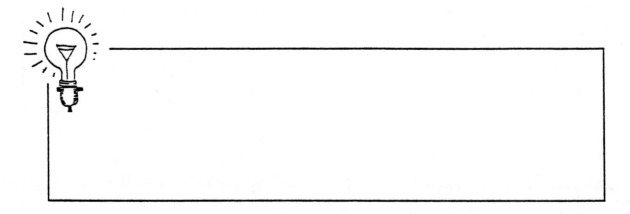

What Are My Best Products

**80% of your sales come from
20% of what you offer!**

Customers usually know your major products and services but other important features of your business may not be readily apparent. Think about the total package required to meet the needs of your market. Make a complete list of the products and services offered. Do some sell better than others? Are there any gaps or overlaps in the package?

_____
_____
_____
_____
_____
_____
_____
_____
_____
_____
_____
_____

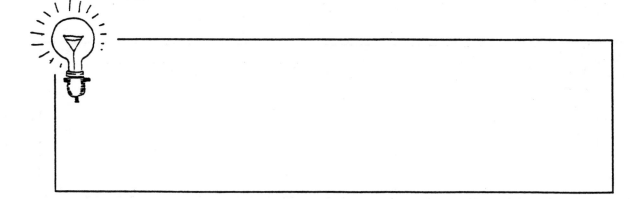

Step IV:
Use Your Marketing Mix
to Satisfy Customer Needs

COMPONENTS

PRODUCTS & SERVICES
What's unique about your products and services? Do they fill the needs of your targeted clientele? Is there too much or too little of anything? Do some things sell better than others?

DISTRIBUTION
Does your distribution system really fill your needs? Is it economical? Is your objective to wholesale, retail or both? What's entailed?

PRICING
Are you adequately covering costs? Are your prices fair both to you and your customers? How do they compare with competitor prices? Do you review prices regularly?

PROMOTION & ADVERTISING
Are you getting the most mileage from promotional dollars? Have you covered the basics well enough (name, logo, signs, etc.)? Have you asked people for feedback about your image and the effectiveness of your promotion?

The marketing mix is like a jigsaw puzzle with four major parts interconnecting to create the final picture. We provide a detailed description of these parts in the next section. The important thing to remember is that **every company has a different mix.** Your job is to figure out how yours goes together.

YOU CAN ALWAYS CHANGE THE MIX!

marketing mix

PART I:
Products & Services

Let's face it, people want the most for their money. "The best product at the best price" is a phrase heard often and taken seriously. Recognizing this, micro businesses can specialize in high quality products and services. They can guarantee their customers the **best** at reasonable prices.

As a rule, always try to provide the finest product or service. Learn all you can about your trade; study new methods of production or the latest techniques in your field. Focus on what's special about your business and make the most of it!

Remember, whatever you offer should fill **real** customer needs. Follow sales trends, and be aware of shifts in those needs. Be flexible enough to make changes as the market dictates. Understand the "life cycle" of your product lines or service — a new item may sell poorly at first, pick up as its reputation grows, then eventually decline. Keep sales moving by anticipating ups and downs in customer demands.

BE PROUD OF WHAT YOU DO, AND HOW YOU DO IT!

Something unique about self-employed people is the high level of quality and expertise which prevails in their enterprises. Most self-employed people get into business because they like making a product or providing a service or selling something special.

Carefully consider your 20% best products and services. No one wants you to tie up capital in slow-moving merchandise that fills neither the customer's nor your own needs.

marketing mix

PART II:
Distribution

Your options for distribution are usually either direct sales to the consumer (retailing) or the use of a "middleman" (wholesaling). The type of business often dictates the system used. There are pros and cons to both.

Periodically evaluate the effectiveness and efficiency of your distribution system. Changes in customer buying habits, company rules, retailing techniques, competitors' methods and other business trends could require you to make adjustments. Experiment with different methods to see which bring the best results.

RETAILING is selling directly to the consumer. It gives you a higher profit margin and has the advantage that you keep control of the marketing. The disadvantages often include higher overhead and capital tied up in slow-moving merchandise. It can mean that you start small and stay small longer.

WHOLESALING relieves you of some marketing work, but cuts into your profits. To wholesale you have to produce more product for less money. The emphasis is on volume. This can be a problem for those who take pride in producing finely crafted one-of-a-kind items.

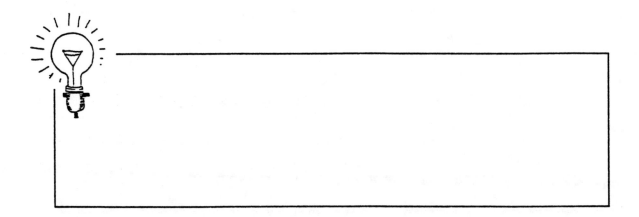

SOME OPTIONS FOR DISTRIBUTION

WHOLESALER

This is someone who purchases large quantities of merchandise at a discount price. S/he stores, handles and sells the material, relieving you of those responsibilities. This lessens your profit but saves you time and effort.

_____

_____

MANUFACTURER'S REPRESENTATIVE

This is someone who sells on commission as an agent for different clients with similar product lines. You still do the shipping, billing and collecting. Your profit margin will be a little higher.

_____

_____

CONSIGNMENT

This is selling goods through a small store or retailer for commission. In this way, you can test customer response to a product before committing yourself to it in earnest. You do tie up some money, and to be effective, you need to find the right store(s) and have adequate displace space.

_____

_____

Whichever system you choose, develop a friendly working relationship with your distributor. Provide dependable products and furnish advertising displays.

marketing mix

PART III:
Pricing

Determining fair prices can be tough! The idea is to cover costs and make a profit while attracting customers and building volume. Prices must be competitive and within the customer's reach. In setting them, consider the **minimum** you need to take out of the business for living expenses.

The uniqueness of what you offer is an important factor in setting prices. The more distinctive your business and the more customer attention you give, the more flexibility you'll have in pricing. A store that offers guarantees, credit and personalized service can usually charge more for its products.

PRICES MUST BE FAIR TO <u>BOTH</u>!

Do you regularly review prices? How do they compare with those of your competitors? Are you covering costs and making a profit?

ELEMENTS OF PRICING

FIXED COSTS are the expenses of the workplace: electricity, heat, telephone, salaries, machinery, etc. They are basically the same regardless of your volume.

VARIABLE COSTS are those which fluctuate according to how much business you do: materials, machinery maintenance, unexpected breakdowns, markdowns or defective goods.

PROFIT is a planned, integral part of your price. Without it, your business cannot survive or grow!

"DOWNHOME" PRICING FORMULA

Cost of materials + labor (at the rate it would cost to pay someone to replace you) + 40% of the labor-plus-materials figure + 10% of the labor-plus-materials figure for overhead x 2 = RETAIL PRICE. Then, throw the whole thing out and figure out what you can get for it!

Adapted from: *Homemade Money* by Barbara Brabec (Betterway Publications, 1984)

Applying pricing formulas may be fun, but is often impractical. The retail price still has to be adjusted to the market. In the end, common sense must prevail.

Experiment with different pricing schemes. Ask your customers how they feel about your prices and seek their constructive advice.

marketing mix

PART IV:

Promotion & Advertising

These two work together to build awareness of your product or service, to stimulate sales and to establish a favorable image of your company. By carefully emphasizing your business strengths, you can build a promotional effort of lasting value.

PROMOTION deals with the generalities of "popularizing" your business operation as a whole. It helps you establish an overall image for your enterprise and informs the public of what you offer.

ADVERTISING (according to the dictionary) "proclaims the qualities or advantages of a product." Its purpose is to sell a particular product or service.

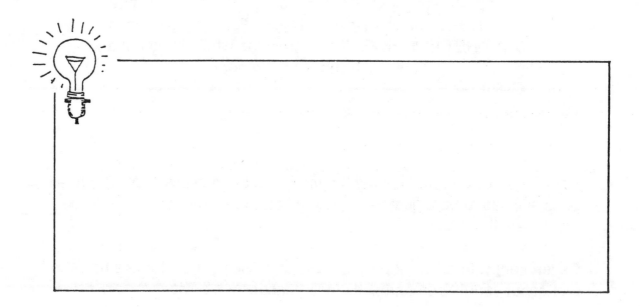

ALWAYS PUT YOUR BEST FOOT FORWARD!

Be sure to measure the effectiveness of your promotion and advertising.
Ask customers how they found out about you. Try coupons. Advertise
different specials at different times, in different areas and in
different ways — and compare the results.

Overall Promotion to Build an Image

The specifics of how you build an image will depend upon your overall goals and directions. The sheep farmer who specializes in producing lambs for the Easter market projects one image, whereas another who also markets fleeces, spins wool and knits clothing projects a different image.

In building an image, your name and logo are very important. Your store appearance, the type of people working for you, the way the telephone is answered and the way your printed materials are presented are also considerations. Get into the habit of doing things well to reinforce the **positive** word-of-mouth about you.

WHAT'S MY IMAGE?

	Yes	No
Does my business fit into the surrounding area?	☐	☐
Is my location visible and accessible?	☐	☐
Is my sign simple and appealing?	☐	☐
Are the premises orderly and inviting?	☐	☐
Is the merchandise well presented?	☐	☐
Are my salespeople friendly and knowledgeable?	☐	☐
Do my customers remember my business favorably?	☐	☐

Be active in the community. If you're a service provider, you might give educational talks related to your field. If you're a small manufacturer, you might sponsor a town softball team. If you're a craftsperson, you might give demonstrations in schools or at the annual town fair. Well-planned promotional techniques help you build credibility and gain respect.

Customer Attention

Personalized customer service is one of the micro businessperson's greatest strengths. Develop a friendly, helpful relationship with your customers and learn their names as a courtesy. Have your salespeople do the same — in the shop, on the road and over the phone. These details create a lasting impression in the customer's mind.

FIXED, CONSISTENT BUSINESS HOURS ARE ESSENTIAL

Your Name, Slogan & Logo

Look around at the great ideas people have for identifying their businesses. Does your name and logo convey the image you want?

THE NAME

If you are picking a name for the first time or changing names, put together a long list of ideas from which to choose. Names that are too cute, too hard to say, too long to use on signs, business cards and on the phone don't work well. The name must convey not only the type of business, but also imply the degree of formality. Take enough time to make the right choice.

THE SLOGAN

A slogan helps round out the name and clarify what the business is about. If you use your own name as the business name, a slogan becomes particularly important. Consider these . . .

ALLEN & SMITH
We've got glass

CHARLES BROWN
Darn good carpenter. Very handy person.

ACME PLUMBING
Where a flush always beats a full house

Ideally, your business name and slogan will reflect your uniqueness and distinguish you from your competitors. It will be general enough to cover what you do now and in the foreseeable future. Brainstorm with a group of friends to come up with the right combination.

THE LOGO

A logo is a symbol which represents your business. It's short for "logotype" which, to a printer, is a single piece of type bearing two or more usually separate elements. The logo helps reinforce the customer's positive experience in your shop.

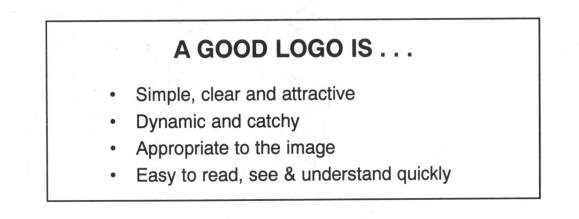

A GOOD LOGO IS . . .

- Simple, clear and attractive
- Dynamic and catchy
- Appropriate to the image
- Easy to read, see & understand quickly

The logo must be designed in such a way that it can be used in a variety of ways — on signs, vehicles, handbills, newspaper ads, business cards, postcards, catalogues, brochures, stationery, invoices, etc. Some businesses even develop two variations of the same logo for different applications. Have a graphic artist help you design the logo. It's worth the investment for an eye-catching, appropriate design.

THE MAINE IDEA
SUCCESSFUL SELF-EMPLOYMENT

Your Location

The accessibility and visibility of your location are major considerations. The best location will strike a balance between business possibilities and personal considerations (e.g., being close to home). Cost may be a key factor in determining where you locate. What are the pros and cons of your location? Is the business potential really there? If you're in an out-of-the-way place, can you compensate some way?

Your Store or Shop Image

Customers are impressed by a clean, well-organized look. A professional appearance reflects pride and quality and says something about your business.

SIGNS create a first impression and strengthen your company's image in the minds of satisfied customers — inviting them to return. Make it simple, but distinctive. Display it prominently! Your investment will pay off in the long run.

WINDOW DISPLAYS add interest to the business and its products. They are an inexpensive way of introducing new merchandise and advertising special promotions or sales. Develop "themes" for your windows with colorful displays. Get ideas from friends and employees.

OUTSIDE SPACE should be neat and accessible. Your surroundings contribute to the attractiveness of what you sell. Shopping at your business should be as easy and comfortable as possible.

INSIDE SPACE, when it's neat and conveniently organized, encourages customers to look at everything you are offering. Well-prepared displays highlight your products. Use bright colors, easy-to-read signs and adequate lighting.

Your Out-of-Shop Image

BUSINESS CARDS are a convenient way of helping people remember your name and location. Design a card that stands out. Use a picture or logo, and various colors. Fold-over business cards have the advantage of giving you more space for your message. Cards are an inexpensive way to promote throughout your marketing area when posted on bulletin boards, cash registers, etc.

BROCHURES explain the uniqueness of a business and its products. For certain types of businesses, they are a particularly valuable way of highlighting important aspects of the operation. A brochure can enhance your estimate or price quote.

VEHICLE ADVERTISING is a reasonable way of keeping your name in front of the public. A nicely painted and lettered truck is always helpful to your image. Magnetic signs are both attractive and removable. If you do service work, also consider using a sandwich board outside the job site: "Chimney sweeping by Rocky's Wood Heat Co." People will take notice and remember your name.

TRADE SHOWS AND FAIRS are often a good chance to display your wares and reach potential customers. Carefully pick events that are appropriate to your business and offer maximum customer exposure.

DO THE SIMPLE, INEXPENSIVE THINGS FIRST!

NEWSPAPER ARTICLES are extremely valuable ways of promoting your business. Local newspapers are often interested in stories about local folks, new businesses in town, unusual occupations and the like. Suggest to a reporter that s/he do a story about you. Help the reporter get the facts straight by writing a news release which stresses the unique features of your business. Provide a high quality black-and-white photo to accompany the story.

Many micro businesspeople **do** have interesting stories about how they produce their products and their plans for expansion. A wire service picked up a local article about a friend of ours who makes soapstone bed warmers. They published it nationwide and he started getting orders from everywhere!

Advertising & Special Promotions

The objective is to move as much merchandise (or services) as possible as inexpensively as possible.

SOME PRINCIPLES

- Establish a **fixed** advertising budget proportionate to the size of your business. Consider using a percentage (at least 2–3%) of either your current estimated or last year's gross sales.

- Use simple, inexpensive promotional techniques first; then work progressively into more complex, expensive undertakings.

- Capture the fullest possible share of the market **when the market is there.** As a rule, advertise at peak sales times, not when you're in a slump.

- Always advertise your **best** products, not the slow movers. Analyze the 80/20 rule to determine which products are most likely to move and bring the desired return.

- When something works, stick with it! Compare cost with results.

- Know your customers. Remember whom you're targeting. It will help you decide where and how to advertise.

- Shop around for your best advertising dollar!

How to Get Started!

1st Carefully select the products or services to be offered and determine the real customer benefits to be stressed.

2nd Set **realistic** goals and sales projections in order to measure the success of your efforts.

3rd Develop an overall plan of action and a timetable that includes all the various types of advertising to be used.

4th Prepare a tight budget and watch it closely.

BE CAREFUL TO USE LIMITED RESOURCES WISELY!

Some Advertising Options

THRIFTY ADVERTISING such as swap guides, "shoppers" (giveaway fliers), church bulletins, etc., are often effective and inexpensive. Be inventive in finding ways of getting the word out about your business. Be sure thrifty advertising achieves your overall purposes and is consistent with the image you are trying to project.

SPECIAL MAILINGS can be particularly effective with your best customers and "hot" prospects. Carefully develop your mailing list. Keep a sign-up sheet near the cash register: "If you give us your name and address, we'll be glad to let you know of special sales." Put a jar of beans on the counter and offer a prize to the person who comes closest to guessing the right number (a good way to gather names and addresses).

Anyone with whom you've had direct contact is a "hot" prospect. Since the rate of return on "cold" prospects is very low, we suggest targeting your mailings only to your very best customers. When possible, add a personal touch like a handwritten note.

YELLOW PAGES, according to most of our clients, can be helpful in the first year or two of operations. Thereafter, just having your name in **bold** print under the appropriate categories may be enough.

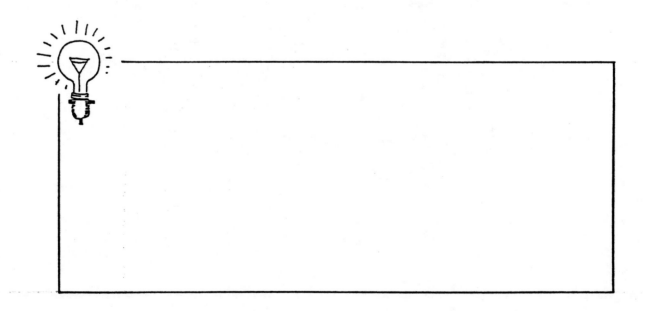

NEWSPAPERS, both dailies and weeklies, are commonly used by micro businesses to advertise. Local newspapers provide good exposure for those servicing a limited area. A small ad **repeated often** is usually more effective than a larger one run infrequently. Many newspapers give their regular advertisers special discount prices. Check with your suppliers about "co-op advertising" in which they pay part of the cost.

MAGAZINES, particularly if they have wide circulations, have expensive advertising rates. Many people squander limited resources trying to "make it big." Smaller, more local publications may be better for micro businesses; try your specialty trade or business association publication.

RADIO can be very effective for certain types of advertising, but the costs mount up rapidly. Know your targeted customers well before you try it. Frequency and timing are important: many package deals are for "off" hours that may not meet your needs. Consider recording your own ad to give people a chance to hear your voice. Also, since folks listening to the radio frequently can't write down a telephone number, providing a visual association can be helpful: "Next to the post office" or "Right downtown on Main St." or "Check the yellow pages under plumbers."

TELEVISION is too costly for most micro businesses, but sometimes cooperative advertising packages make it possible. We get mixed responses about its effectiveness from those who have tried it.

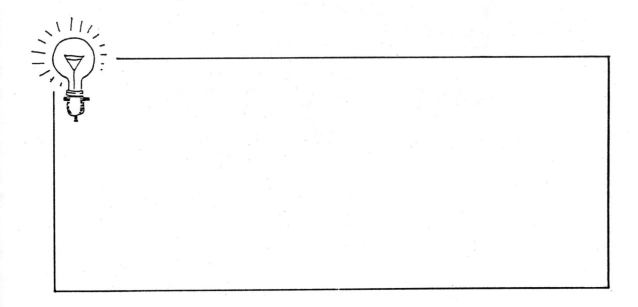

Guidelines for Ads

A GOOD AD DEMONSTRATES THE CUSTOMER BENEFIT!

Creating an advertisement involves writing the copy, selecting the illustration, preparing the layout and making arrangements with the selected media. The copy is all the written or spoken material. Illustrations should be selected for the interest they create and their appropriateness. The layout is the way the various elements are arranged and is important in guiding the reader's eye in an orderly fashion.

Carefully design your ads to attract attention and develop public interest. Common sense, good taste and, above all, **honesty** should prevail in their design and content.

PRINCIPLES OF AD DESIGN

- Show how the customer benefits by buying from you.
- Emphasize only a **few** important points.
- Feature certain items, and give a price or price range.
- Keep the wording short and simple.
- Use humor sparingly, if at all.
- Clearly state your name, address and phone number.
- Pick a straightforward layout with an illustration.

PUTTING YOUR AD TOGETHER...

1st Decide what you *really* want to say, and rough out the text to see how it reads.

2nd Then eliminate what you can without cutting important information. Get to the point!

3rd Select a few options for illustrations. Pictures or graphics add interest and enhance your image.

4th Put all the pieces together in different layouts. What does the reader "see"? How does the ad flow?

5th Test the layouts with friends and acquaintances to pick the best one.

The media people you deal with are usually happy to make suggestions. Your suppliers may also have good ideas.

Mapping Out a Basic Promotional Plan
A Four-Step Worksheet

LOOK IN-HOUSE FIRST
What needs to be done in-house to clean up the physical space and improve customer attention? (Clean, paint, organize, improve displays or signage, employee training, etc.)

_____

_____

_____

_____

SIMPLE, EASY THINGS
What promotional tasks are either so simple and easy or so basic to the overall promotional effort that they can't be overlooked? (Appealing logo, interesting business cards, fliers, brochure, vehicle signs, educational talks, news releases, etc.)

_____

_____

_____

_____

FOCUS ON 20% BEST BUYERS
How can you best target the 20% best customers? (Develop a mailing list, personal notes or letters, special sales or offerings, etc.)

_____

_____

_____

_____

GETTING MORE AMBITIOUS
When you formally advertise, what is most likely to produce results for your business? (Weekly or daily newspapers, yellow pages, magazines, radio, T.V., etc.) What specific products, services and customer benefits will be featured?

_____

_____

_____

PROJECT AN IMAGE BASED ON YOUR STRENGTHS

Six-Month Promotional Plan
(TO BE REVISED & REPROJECTED EVERY THREE MONTHS)

GOALS & OBJECTIVES (Be as specific as possible)	SPECIFIC PROMOTIONAL	
	MONTH OF:	MONTH OF:

HAVE YOU PRECISELY DETERMINED CUSTOMER NEEDS, COMPETITIVE

Business Name: _____

Period Covered: _____ to _____

| & MARKETING ACTIVITIES | | ✔ | FINAL RESULTS (...and observations) |
MONTH OF:	FOLLOWING 3 MONTHS OF:		

ADVANTAGES, THE TARGETED MARKET AND THE MARKETING MIX?

Remember, your goal is to build a large pool of satisfied customers who have confidence in your company and come back again and again. These folks will be your best advertising. Give them the customer attention they deserve.

WHEN TIMES ARE TOUGH, YOU'VE GOT TO USE ALL YOUR RESOURCES TO STAY ON YOUR FEET

You're in business to make a profit. To do this, your finances must be properly organized. Before you can plan where you're going, you must know where you've been and how you got there.

Recordkeeping is based on common sense and provides vital business information. Through analysis of your records, you can clearly see how much money was taken in and how much was spent. Accurate records give you an indication of what to expect in the future. Because it makes you more cost conscious, recordkeeping is the best way to cut expenses in a business.

Effective recordkeeping (when combined with conscientious monthly analysis) will give you the information needed to make decisions about the future of your business. It will help you trim costs, save on income taxes, keep track of payroll records, sales tax and much more.

It is only by taking firm control of the financial aspect that you will be able to turn a high quality product or service into a thriving, stable business. The simple discipline of recordkeeping will make you a more effective manager.

Everyone we talk to agrees that these tools are needed: a reliable system for recording daily financial transactions, a good accountant who understands your needs, cash flow projections and monthly analysis of your real situation. Conscientious use of these tools produces a smoother functioning enterprise. You'll be able to analyze your financial situation with greater accuracy and expand with confidence, knowing you're in control.

ANY STEP YOU TAKE IS A STEP IN THE RIGHT DIRECTION!

Section Three:

Basic Finances

Steps to Financial Control

STEP I:

GET THE RIGHT OUTSIDE HELP

A banker, an accountant, a lawyer. . . a candle stick maker.

STEP II:

SET UP A BOOKKEEPING SYSTEM THAT WORKS

It's basic to being in business for yourself and a fairly simple matter for the typical sole proprietor.

STEP III:

KEEP FOCUSED ON THE BOTTOM LINE

Cash flow projections and analysis alert you to potential problems well in advance.

STEP IV:

USE THE OTHER TOOLS OF THE TRADE

The Balance Sheet and Profit & Loss explain the business' financial situation and help you understand it better.

STEP V:

TAKE OTHER MEASURES TO TIGHTEN UP

Customer credit, inventory control, purchasing procedures, etc., are all important to running a smooth operation.

My Overall Financial Needs

HANG IN THERE!

A CHECKLIST

	Right NOW	6 Mos. Later
AN ACCOUNTANT... ...who truly understands my situation. ...who gives my work the priority it deserves.		
A BOOKKEEPING SYSTEM... ...I can understand and be comfortable with. ...that is appropriate to my situation. ...that separates my personal and business expenses.		
INCOME & EXPENSE PLANNING		
MONTHLY FINANCIAL ANALYSIS... ...regular business meetings ...Balance Sheet and Profit & Loss statements ...comparison of real and projected cash flow		
A COLLECTION SYSTEM... ...a written credit policy ...timely billings and collections		
INVENTORY CONTROL		
STANDARD PURCHASING PROCEDURES		
TAX CONTROL AND PLANNING		
BETTER BANKING RELATIONSHIPS		

Step I:
Get the Right Outside Help

Bankers

Bankers and banks are all different. Some take the interests of the small operator seriously, others don't. If you are lucky enough to find the right banker, s/he can be a tremendous resource.

Bankers are good at financial analysis. They are familiar with cash flow projections and should be able to advise you on yours. Bankers can often provide valuable information on...

- General economic conditions.

- Regional and industry trends.

- Marketing and new product opportunities.

- Leads to other financial and non-financial help (including introductions & references when needed).

- Credit checks and information on customers and suppliers.

Your banker can help you see how your business fits in and will, ideally, have a vested interest in your success.

Bankers are also helpful in assessing credit patterns in your area. Consumer credit payments tend to lag around Christmas, pick up as tax refunds are distributed, and then fall off again during the summer. Knowing this, you can plan accordingly. Get your banker's advice on your credit policy. S/he can explain how credit cards may be an attractive alternative to actually offering credit yourself.

SHOP AROUND UNTIL YOU FIND A BANK YOU LIKE!

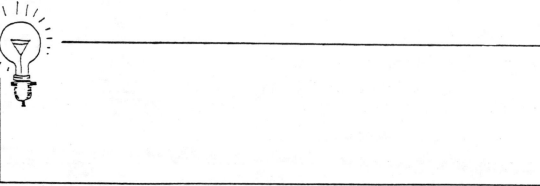

Accountants

An accountant can save you time, energy and money — and strengthen your self-confidence to manage the business. Accountants are trained to advise you on taxes, financial systems and special bookkeeping problems. They can help you...

- Set up systems and controls.

- Prepare and analyze cash flow statements.

- Deal with personnel and business taxes.

- Prepare credit applications.

- Find sources of financing.

Shop around for the right accountant for you and your business. Compare fees, services and quality. Find someone you feel comfortable with and check references before making a final decision. Does s/he work with other micro businesses? Are they pleased with him/her?

Some accountants charge by the hour (or fraction thereof) while others prefer a monthly retainer. Whichever your accountant requires, know what you're paying for and be sure your needs are being met. Don't waste money having the accountant do things you can learn to do yourself — keep accurate, up-to-date records. After setting up a bookkeeping system, learn to use it in monitoring your business' growth.

MAKE YOUR ACCOUNTANT PART OF THE TEAM!

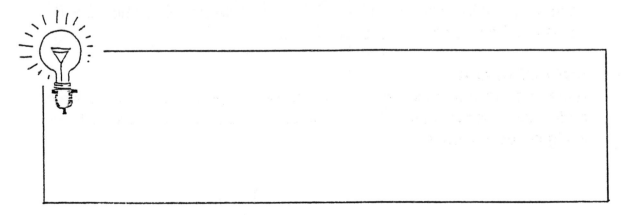

Options for Legal Structure

Every business has a structure for tax and legal purposes. It's important to consider yours since it will influence aspects of your management. Will you be structured as a sole proprietorship, a partnership or a corporation? Each legal structure has pros and cons depending on the size and type of business, and the number of people involved in managing or financing it.

KEY QUESTIONS

- How much management control do you want?
- How much capital is needed and what's the liability?
- What's the best way to minimize taxes?
- What happens if you die or become disabled?

STRUCTURAL OPTIONS

SOLE PROPRIETORSHIPS
Most small businesses are organized as sole proprietorships because it's a structure that is flexible and readily meets a wide variety of needs.

PARTNERSHIPS
They can be based on a simple understanding between the partners, but they have a bad track record and usually don't last for long. With the help of a lawyer, you can be spared some of the major headaches that come up in partnerships. It's best to have a written understanding which clearly spells out the responsibilities of each person.

CORPORATIONS
A major disadvantage in setting up a corporation is cost and the hassle of additional paperwork (including double entry bookkeeping). Legal advice is highly recommended.

	ADVANTAGES	DISADVANTAGES
Sole Proprietorship The simplest type of business. It is owned by one person who assumes the risks to the extent of ALL his/her assets. Only the owner can make binding business decisions.	It's simply organized and flexible. There is no profit distribution and only minimal legal restrictions. It can be simply discontinued at any time.	The owner has unlimited liability and it is difficult to obtain adequate working capital. Skill and knowledge is generally limited to that of the owner.
Partnership Owned by two or more persons who pool their resources and share the risks. Each person contributes time, money, property and/or skills.	It's simply organized and has greater financial strength than the sole proprietorship. Partners share a strong personal interest in the business, providing a better base of skill and knowledge.	The owners still have unlimited liability. Divided decision making can lead to misunderstandings and conflict. Death dissolves the partnership.
Corporation An entity with rights and duties of its own, separate from its owners. Owners are stockholders; managers may or may not be.	The business has an unlimited life. Individual liability is limited. There is greater financial strength; more varied skill and knowledge. The structure is readily adapted to the growing business; ownership is easily transferred.	It is more difficult and expensive to organize. The activities are restricted by charter. It is subject to special taxation in addition to many state and federal controls.

BE OPEN TO OUTSIDE HELP AND
USE COMMUNITY RESOURCES

THINK ABOUT YOUR BUSINESS ASSISTANCE NEEDS. Could you use the help of an accountant, lawyer, banker, marketing advisor, management counselor, technician, etc.? Where will you find such help?

_____

_____

_____

_____

Your local library, chamber of commerce or service organization (Rotary, Kiwanis, etc.) may know sources of assistance in your area. If not, check with state government agencies and the Small Business Administration.

Step II:

Set Up a Bookkeeping System that Works

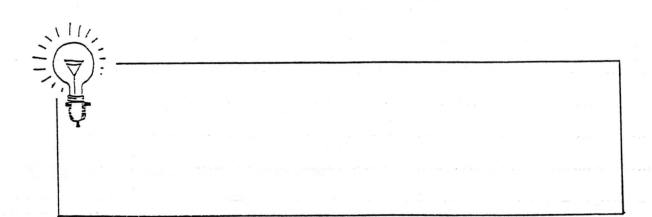

Perhaps you're like many others who think that bookkeeping is simply keeping your receipts in a shoebox 'til tax time! Many businesses that thrive today started that way, but somewhere along the line, a more reliable way of keeping track of money was established.

Any growing company eventually comes to a point where management and bookkeeping become an essential part of making a profit. To run a profitable business, there are certain things you need to know with reasonable accuracy — which expenses can be deducted from your income taxes, how much your overhead is, how much you're taking out for living expenses, what you're spending on materials and supplies, etc. Without a bookkeeping system, it's impossible to control these outlays.

Do consult with an accountant before committing yourself to any bookkeeping system. Be sure the system you choose is appropriate to your needs. By getting set up properly from the start, you will save time later.

On the next few pages, we present the two most common "single entry" bookkeeping systems used by micro businesses. They both operate on exactly the same principle, but approach it in different ways. The most rudimentary system is an Income Ledger, a business checkbook and an Expenditure Ledger. The "one-write" bookkeeping system is a bit more elaborate and costs more to set up, but has many advantages.

RECIPE FOR BASIC BOOKKEEPING

Ingredients:

(1) BUSINESS CHECKBOOK

(1) INCOME LEDGER*

(1) EXPENDITURE LEDGER*

(1) INTERESTED OWNER/MANAGER

* A **ledger** is a book in which the monetary transactions of a business are posted.

NOT A BAD RECIPE!

THE FINAL INGREDIENT IS YOU!

BETTER FINANCIAL CONTROL

Tim Sample

Business Checkbook

This is an essential part of getting yourself organized and "being in business." It helps separate your personal and business expenses — which is vital if you are to keep track of the money flowing into and out of your business. Using your personal checkbook is not good enough. If you fail to separate business and personal expenses, you'll never know how well your business is doing and you'll complicate your life at tax time (and probably lose legitimate deductions).

No matter how small your company, having a separate business checkbook to handle business accounts is essential in planning for growth and controlling expenses. One major advantage of a business checkbook is larger checks and stubs which give you more space to write and do calculations.

Keep track of any money taken out of the business. Rather than taking cash, write yourself a check. That way, you'll always know exactly how much you've taken each week or month...and maybe you'll be motivated to cut back on unnecessary personal expenses.

SEPARATE YOUR PERSONAL & BUSINESS EXPENSES!

Income Ledger

As a record of business income, the Income Ledger is a detailed, daily listing of all incoming cash from sales, collections on accounts and other sources. You'll need this information for tax purposes, but the Income Ledger can also help you manage better. As a control mechanism, it can help you identify your best customers and your best-selling products or product lines.

The Income Ledger needn't be terribly elaborate. Use a notebook or some lined paper for it. Organize your receipts in categories which help you analyze the success of your sales efforts and planning. A simple journal will look something like this:

SMITH & SMITH SUPPLY CO.

DATE	RECEIVED FROM	TAXABLE SALES			SALES TAX		NON-TAXABLE SALES		TOTAL SALES	
	cash sales		10 50			53				11 03
	D. Baker—pd. on acct.		25 —							25 —
	Steve's Electric	2 25 —				11 25			2 36 25	
	cash sales		22 30			1 11				23 41
	H. Brown—service call							20 —		20 —
	cash sales		16 40			82				17 22
	R&R Construction	1 90 —				9 50			1 99 50	

Expenditure Ledger

This is simply a ruled piece of paper with enough columns to break down your expenses into categories or "accounts." Pads of ledger paper can be purchased at any stationery store for this purpose.

A good deal of thought needs to go into determining those expense categories which fill your needs. Those you select will be used over and over gain in your recordkeeping and analysis. You'll use them not only for the Expenditure Ledger, but also to set up your Cash Flow Projection, Profit & Loss Statement and Balance Sheet. You should become so familiar with these accounts that they are second nature to you.

TYPICAL EXPENSE CATEGORIES

Check those you need!

☐ Raw Material/Merchandise   ☐ Telephone
☐ Owner's Drawings   ☐ Postage
☐ Salaries   ☐ Freight
☐ Payroll Taxes & Benefits   ☐ Business Supplies
☐ Subcontractors   ☐ Repairs/Maintenance
☐ Professional Services   ☐ Dues & Publications
☐ Advertising Expense   ☐ Insurance
☐ Car/Truck Expenses*   ☐ Taxes/Licenses
☐ Building Expenses/Improvements*   ☐ Interest Paid/Bank Charges
☐ Equipment Purchase*   ☐ Miscellaneous
☐ Rent   ☐ Telephone
☐ Utilities   ☐ Other:

*Purchases of equipment, vehicles or furniture are generally depreciated over time.

HAVE YOUR ACCOUNTANT REVIEW YOUR WORK!

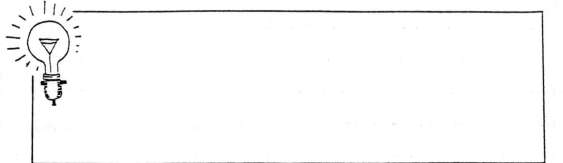

RECORDKEEPING IS THE BEST WAY TO CUT EXPENSES

The final ingredient in our recipe for basic bookkeeping is **you**, the owner/manager. Without your active interest and concern, no recordkeeping system can be very useful. The financial management of your business is not to be delegated or forgotten. Stay on top of things! Once a system is set up, use it to see how you are spending money and to think of ways to cut costs.

Expenditure Ledger

Smith's DownHome

						1		2		3	
DATE	CHECK NO.	TO WHOM		TOTAL		STORE MERCHANDISE		REMODELING SUPPLIES		OWNER'S DRAWINGS	
4/2	224	Builder's Supply, Inc.		86	50			86	50		
4/4	225	Downtown Associates		350	00						
4/4	226	Harry's Lawn Care		10	00						
4/5	227	Helen Smith		250	00					250	00
4/8	228	Anywhereville Electric		42	25						
4/8	229	Bring Your Own Telephone Co.		127	49						
4/9	230	Best Insurance Co.		65	70						
4/12	231	Builder's Supply, Inc.		272	00			249	50		
4/12	232	Joe Smith		250	00					250	00
4/12	233	You Name It Lumber & Supply		396	32			337	42		
4/12	234	Builder's Supply, Inc.		126	40						
4/13	235	Tom's Electric		152	72						
4/14	236	Joe Good Accounting Service		50	00						
4/14	237	Smalltown Auto & Truck Service		94	74						
4/14	238	Anywhereville Post Office		24	30						
4/16	239	B & D Equipment Co.		237	40						
4/16	240	Gas Credit Card, Inc.		270	92						
4/16	241	Helen Smith		200	00					200	00
4/21	242	Royal Printing Service		76	20						
4/21	243	Smalltown Chamber of Commerce		75	00						
4/21	244	The Daily Telegram		110	25						
4/22	245	Builder's Supply, Inc.		496	20			480	50		
4/22	246	Acme Plumbing		229	95						
4/25	247	Big & Big Appliances, Inc.		592	65	592	65				
4/26	248	Helen Smith		220	00					220	00
4/27	249	Anywhereville Post Office		35	10						
4/27	250	Big John's Freight Co.		54	60						
4/29	251	Bean, Burnhim & Bitehim, Attnys.		90	00						
		TOTAL		4986	69	592	65	1153	92	920	00
			PROF SERVICES			EQUIPMENT		RENT		UTILITIES	
		Miscellaneous Tally	140	00		237	40	350	00	42	25

<u>**AT THE END OF EACH MONTH:**</u>

(1) RULE OFF (2) TALLY UP COLUMNS (3) SEPARATE OUT MISCELLANEOUS ACCOUNTS

USE INFORMATION AS REQUIRED IN CASH FLOW

4 SUB-CONTRACT	5 TRUCK EXPENSES	6 REPAIRS & MAINTENANCE	7 BUSINESS SUPPLIES	8 POSTAGE	9 ADVERTISING	10 MISCELLANEOUS Description	10 MISCELLANEOUS Expenses
						Rent	350 00
		10 00					
						Electric	42 25
						Telephone	127 49
						Insurance	65 70
			22 50				
		58 90					
		126 40					
152 72						Prof. Serv.	50 00
	94 74						
				24 30		Equip.	237 40
	270 92						
					76 20	Dues	75 00
					110 25		
			15 70				
229 95							
				35 10		Freight	54 60
						Prof. Serv.	90 00
382 67	365 66	195 30	38 20	59 40	186 45		1092 44

TELEPHONE	FREIGHT	DUES & PUBLICATIONS	INSURANCE				
127 49	54 60	75 00	65 70				

						TOTAL EXPENDITURES FOR MONTH	4986 69

(REAL COLUMN), PROFIT & LOSS, BALANCE SHEET

One-Write Bookkeeping

If you write more than 20 checks a month or are thinking of expanding, we strongly recommend looking into the "one-write" system. It's practically automatic bookkeeping, and can save you time and money.

The major advantage of the one-write is that you use one book for everything! You don't need a separate checkbook, expenditure ledger and payroll book. All the work is done in one place, which saves confusion and assures greater accuracy. Many micro business people we know find the one-write bookkeeping system ideally suited to their needs.

It's easy to use! It consists of checks (printed to your specifications) with a strip of carbon on the back. (Any bank will accept these checks.) When you write a check, the information is automatically recorded on your Expenditure Ledger (saving you the trouble of transferring figures from check to check stub to ledger, etc.). Later, you can break down the original entry information into the expense categories you have devised in the same ledger.

One-write systems are sold under several brand names (ask your accountant or other business people for referrals). A simple start up package costs about $100.

Step III:

Keep Focused
on the Bottom Line

EFFECTIVE MANAGEMENT IS MORE THAN REACTING TO PROBLEMS AND CIRCUMSTANCES

A Cash Flow Projection Tells You How Much Cash is Needed, When It Will Be Needed, and Where It Will Come From!

A Cash Flow Projection with monthly analysis is the best way we know of for focusing on "the bottom line." It shows, month by month, when and how much money will flow into and out of your business. It forewarns you of possible cash problems. Working together with the Cash Flow, a monthly Balance Sheet and Profit & Loss Statement will tell you where your financial strength is and how you've gotten where you are.

Make a habit of doing your financial analysis in a timely manner (preferably during the first five days of the month), and discuss the results with your accountant and/or business associates.

Do you project your cash flow at least three months in advance? Do you compare your projected expenses against your real expenses on a monthly basis?

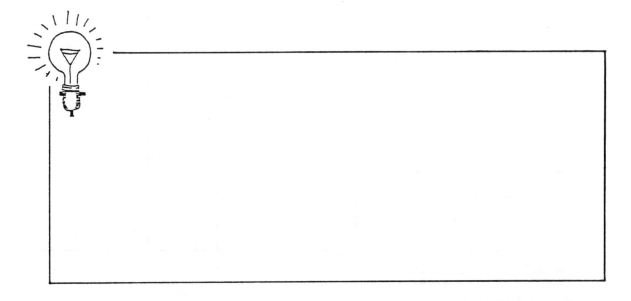

EVERYBODY SHOULD HAVE SOME WAY OF KEEPING TRACK OF MONEY COMING IN AND OUT. NO EXCUSES!

Monthly Expense Worksheet

	HIGH	LOW	MEDIAN	OBSERVATIONS
Raw Materials/Merchandise				
Owner's Draws				
Salaries				
Payroll Taxes & Benefits				
Subcontractors				
Professional Services				
Advertising				
Car/Truck Expenses				
Rent				
Utilities				
Telephone				
Postage				
Freight				
Business Supplies				
Repairs & Maintenance				
Dues & Publications				
Insurance				
Taxes/Licenses				
Loan Repayments				
Miscellaneous				
Other:				
_____				
_____				
_____				
TOTAL MONTHLY EXPENSES				
THREE MONTH EXPENSES				
SIX MONTH EXPENSES				

CAREFUL ANALYSIS OF YOUR REAL AND PROJECTED CASH FLOW WILL IMPROVE YOUR CHANCES OF SUCCESS

Projecting Your Cash Flow

Be conservative when you project your Cash Flow. Give yourself a safe margin by projecting low income and high expenses. Of course, the objective is to be precise but, as with any other planning tool, the Cash Flow Projection is only a guide that provides "benchmarks" against which to measure your progress.

Do your projections in pencil so that you can correct and change them as you go along. With practice, you'll learn to project with greater accuracy. Here's how to get started, using the foldout worksheet inside page 91.

1st CAREFULLY EXAMINE THE CHART
Notice that each monthly column is divided into "Projected" and "Real" to facilitate your monthly analysis. The income and expense categories are to be listed to the left. To simplify matters, the Cash Expenditures should correspond with your Expenditure Ledger; the Cash Receipts may correspond with your Income Ledger.

2nd SET MINIMUM CRITERIA & HAVE REALISTIC EXPECTATIONS
You should get to the point where you are projecting a full 12 months in advance, but this may not be practical at first. For a while, you may want to project only three or four months until you get used to the system. As you gain experience, project for longer periods.

It's vital that you give the system a chance to work. You can expect your initial projections to be way off target. It takes most people at least three months to begin seeing results.

3rd GATHER TOGETHER YOUR BOOKS AND PAST RECORDS
If you have past records on which to base your projections, *great!* If not, don't be deterred; you'll just have to do a little more educated guesswork in the first months.

4th GET STARTED — USING PENCIL SO YOU CAN ERASE!

Since they are more straightforward, work up your expenses first. Certain costs such as rent, salaries, etc., will be almost the same every month. Others such as heating will vary according to seasonal and business changes.

Project your Cash Receipts next. Since very few of us know where our money will come from, this can be risky and difficult. Do it anyway! Make educated guesses. It may be helpful to use categories like "100% Certain," and "Balance to Be Obtained." You may need to develop a sales strategy with specific monetary goals. One way or another, you will make certain assumptions about your ability to reach the market. Be sure to record your calculations in a notebook so that you can refer to them later on.

5th TALLY UP THE COLUMNS

Subtract the Total Cash Expenditures from the Total Cash Available to find your Cash Position. (The Cash Position at the end of one month is the Cash on Hand at the beginning of the next.) The Cash Flow forces you to deal with the economic realities of your situation.

THE CASH FLOW PROJECTION HELPS PIN-POINT YOUR OPERATING PRIORITIES!

Cash Flow Projection & Analysis

MONTH OF:		Proj.	Real	Proj.	Real	Proj.	Real	Proj.	Real	Proj.	Real
CASH ON HAND											
R E C E I P T S											
E X P E N D I T U R E S											
TOTAL EXPENDITURES											
ENDING POSITION											

ACCOUNTS PAYABLE (end of month)					

COMPARING YOUR PROJECTED AND REAL CASH SITUATION

BUSINESS NAME: _____

PERIOD COVERED: _____ to_____

Proj.	Real	Proj.	Real	Proj.	Real	Proj.	Real	Proj.	Real	Proj.	Real	Proj.	Real	TOTALS	

HELPS YOU TO BE MORE REALISTIC ABOUT THE FUTURE!

Analysis & Reprojection

At the End of Each Month

1. After you tally up your Expenditure Ledger, transfer the figures to the "Real" column on the Cash Flow.

2. Carefully analyze **major** discrepancies between the real and projected.

> WHAT WERE MY ORIGINAL ASSUMPTIONS?
>
> WAS I TOO OPTIMISTIC?
>
> HOW SHOULD I REPROJECT FOR THE COMING MONTHS —HIGHER, LOWER OR ABOUT THE SAME?

3. Erase and reproject as necessary. (This is why you did it in pencil!)

You may be amazed at the accuracy of your projections after following this process for a few months. Using a Cash Flow in this way **will** forewarn you of coming problems and give you a clearer sense of business trends. It sure beats now knowing where you'll be six months from now!

GIVE IT A THREE-MONTH TRIAL RUN!

A WORD OF CAUTION!

Your Cash Flow is not a substitute for a monthly Profit & Loss Statement and a Balance Sheet. It could, in fact, give you a misleading picture of how well you're doing. To counterbalance some of its shortcomings, complete the "Accounts Payable" space at the bottom of the sheet. This will help you keep track of increases in your debt load.

Step IV:
Use the Other
Tools of the Trade

Balance Sheet and P & L Work Together

These are the basis for financial analysis and decision-making — one of the businessperson's most important tools. Through careful, ongoing analysis of your Balance Sheet and P & L, you can detect weak spots in your operation and work toward improving them. You can get a sense of just how well (or poorly) things are going from month to month. "Can we pay the bills if things don't go as we expect?" "Do the records show that the business is strong enough to qualify for a loan?"

PROFIT & LOSS STATEMENT, also called an Income Statement, is a summary of business transactions over a period of time (usually a month or a year). It shows the difference between your income and your expenses for the period. It helps you analyze how the business got where it is and gives you an idea of what may be expected in the future.

BALANCE SHEET presents the financial picture of a business on a given date — its assets, liabilities (debts) and ownership. It is usually prepared as of the last day of a month and answers the question, "How did we stand financially at that time?" It shows you whether you own the business or whether your creditors do.

COMPARE THEM MONTHLY! CAN YOU SEE ANY PROGRESS? ANY CHANGE FROM NORMAL SHOULD TRIGGER THE QUESTION, "WHY?"

**THE BALANCE SHEET AND P & L
WORK TOGETHER TO HELP YOU MAKE DECISIONS**

Components of the Profit & Loss

The P & L allows you, as manager, to compare your business' sales volume and costs to those of previous months. You can keep track of whether your expenses are increasing or decreasing, and see whether the business is showing a continuous profit.

PUTTING TOGETHER A PROFIT & LOSS

(1) Determine your Total Sales of merchandise or services (from your Income Ledger).

(2) Subtract the Cost of Goods Sold to get the Gross Margin.

(3) Add up all business expenses and subtract them from the Gross Margin to get the Net Profit (or Loss)

COST OF GOODS SOLD is the total price paid for the products sold plus any freight costs. It can be computed by adding the current month's purchases to the beginning inventory for the month (an estimate) and then subtracting the ending inventory for the month.

EXPENSES come directly from your Expenditure Ledger once you've done your monthly tallies. The expense categories will be the same except that you may want to group some items together. In some P & Ls, expenses are divided into "selling expenses" and "general & administrative expenses," which could be helpful in keeping track of your marketing efforts.

Profit & Loss Statement

Company: _____ For Month (Year) Ending: _____

TOTAL SALES: $_____

LESS COST OF GOODS (SERVICES) SOLD:

* _____ $ _____
* _____ $ _____
* _____ $ _____
* _____ $ _____ $ _____

GROSS MARGIN $ _____

LESS EXPENSES:

* _____ $ _____
* _____ $ _____
* _____ $ _____
* _____ $ _____
* _____ $ _____
* _____ $ _____
* _____ $ _____
* _____ $ _____
* _____ $ _____
* _____ $ _____
* _____ $ _____
* _____ $ _____
* _____ $ _____
* _____ $ _____
* _____ $ _____ $ _____

NET PROFIT (LOSS) $ _____

Components of the Balance Sheet

Although certain details may vary, all Balance Sheets contain the same general information. It's called a Balance Sheet because the Total Assets **always equal** the Total Liabilities (debt) plus Your Net Worth (equity).

ASSETS   are anything the business owns that has a monetary value.

LIABILITIES   are the claims of creditors against the assets — the debts.

Too much debt is dangerous; too little could indicate overly cautious financial management that results in lower sales.

CURRENT ASSETS   can be readily converted into dollars through your normal business activity — cash, accounts receivable, inventory, etc.

FIXED ASSETS   have a long-term use in the business — vehicles, equipment, buildings, property, etc. — and are usually not for resale.

CURRENT LIABILITIES   are short-term financial obligations (a year or less) — accounts payable, taxes, wages, notes and bank payments, etc.

FIXED LIABILITIES   are long-term debts or parts of debts that are **not** for payment within a year — equipment or building loans, mortgages, etc.

YOUR NET WORTH (EQUITY)   is simply the assets less the liabilities. It represents your part in the business — what you are due to get back for your time, energy and capital outlay.

Keep your calculations in a notebook where they can't get lost! This will simplify the task of updating the Balance Sheet from month to month.

Balance Sheet

Company: _____   As of (date) _____

ASSETS (owner by the business)

CURRENT:
* Cash on Hand $ _____
* Accounts Receivable $ _____
* Inventory $ _____
* _____ $ _____
* _____ $ _____
* _____ $ _____ $ _____

FIXED:
* Property $ _____
* Equipment $ _____
* _____ $ _____
* _____ $ _____
* _____ $ _____
* _____ $ _____ $ _____

TOTAL $ _____

ASSETS (owner by the business)

CURRENT:
* Accounts Payable $ _____
* Notes Payable $ _____
* _____ $ _____
* _____ $ _____
* _____ $ _____
* _____ $ _____ $ _____

FIXED:
* Mortgage $ _____
* Long Term Loans $ _____
* _____ $ _____
* _____ $ _____
* _____ $ _____ $ _____

YOUR NET WORTH $ _____

TOTAL $ _____

OBSERVATION & ANALYSIS

Your Monthly Analysis
The Management End of Recordkeeping

It's important to do your financial recordkeeping and analysis in a timely manner — preferably during the **first five business days of the month** (right after you get your bank statement). Once you get the hang of it, four to six hours should be enough to tally the books, post your cash flow, draw up a P & L and Balance Sheet and do some overall analysis. Initially, it may take longer and not really tell you anything terribly important. Don't give up!

You will gradually begin seeing trends and getting ideas of how to trim costs. You'll develop a stronger sense of your business' strengths and weaknesses which **will** help you make better decisions about expansion and/or maintenance of your efforts.

THIS IS FINANCIAL MANAGEMENT

Step V:

Take Other Measures to Tighten Up

Tightening Up!

Customer Credit

When you operate on a tight budget, tying up limited working capital in customer credit can be a major problem. Consider the pros and cons. Offering credit may attract new customers and increase sales, but it also may increase costs for bookkeeping, billing, bad debts, etc. You may avoid this either by not offering credit or by only accepting major credit cards.

If you opt for giving credit, be selective about which customers you give it to. You must decide who is worthy of credit and who is not. Cash sales **are** necessary. You **can** turn away business if need be. The real key to not losing your shirt is a sound credit policy.

THE PRINCIPAL COMPONENTS OF GOOD CREDIT POLICY

- Terms and conditions which are clearly expressed verbally and in writing;

- A **signed** application form which commits the customer;

- Careful screening and credit investigation;

- An efficient system for controlling accounts receivable.

TERMS AND CONDITIONS   can be anything you consider practical — you're calling the shots! How much down payment will be required? How much time will be allowed before a late charge is applied?

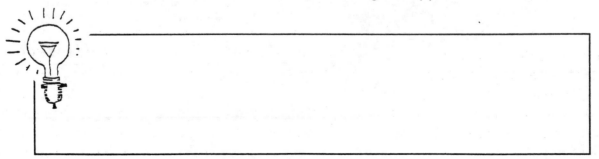

Write a Simple Credit Policy

GENERAL CREDIT AND SERVICE POLICY

Smith's Downhome Electric Works is a family enterprise with limited resources. We emphasize top quality work and materials which meet the latest requirements of the National Electric Code.

TERMS AND CONDITIONS

(1) One-third down payment is required upon initiation of work. The remainer is due when the job is completed.

(2) In the event of a substantial delay between job initiation and completion, interim billing will be necessary.

(3) When credit is extended, the following conditions apply:

    (a) A credit application must be completed and approved prior to work initiation. Credit references will be checked.

    (b) Credit cannot be approved in excess of $500.00.

    (c) Credit shall be allowed for a maximum of 30 days. A discount of 5% shall be granted to customers paying their bill within ten days of work completion.

    (d) In case of non-payment, all additional goods and services will be discontinued and a late charge will be added to the unpaid balance. Additional collection costs and reasonable attorney's fees may also be added.

We appreciate your patronage and hope to continue being of service to you!

Joe & Helen Smith

POST IT AND HAND IT OUT!

CREDIT APPLICATION

DATE: _____

NAME: _____ PHONE: _____

ADDRESS: _____

PREVIOUS ADDRESS: _____

HOW LONG LIVED AT BOTH: PRESENT_____ PREVIOUS _____

OCCUPATION: _____

PLACE OF WORK: _____

HOW LONG WORKED THERE: _____

CREDIT REFERENCES (Name, address, phone)

1. _____

2. _____

3. _____

I understand that in the event payments are not made within the 30 days required, late charges will be added. Collection costs and reasonable attorney's fees will be added to the unpaid balance. If delinquent, repossession of durable goods may be done at will and without notification.

_____

Customer Signature

CREDIT APPROVED SUBJECT TO THE FOLLOWING CONDITIONS:

_____

_____

When you analyze the completed credit application, try to determine the applicant's stability. Check references and find out what you can about the person's character. Look for inconsistencies.

The Matter of Collections

No matter how hard you try, there will always be slow-paying customers who drain your working capital. To speed up collections, invoice promptly, keep the terms tight and have an effective follow-up system. Your best collection process is in-house. Remember, slow-paying customers have interest-free use of your money!

An **Aging Statement** is useful for keeping track of receivables. It simply lists all of the accounts overdue in three columns — 30 days, 60 days, and 90 days. Some effort should be made to collect from each person on the list — a new billing, a personal letter, a phone call, etc. This is one way of planning and controlling collection efforts.

Be prompt in initiating collection. When the terms are set, payment is due. If you wait longer, customers may think you don't care or aren't paying attention. The older your receivables get (60–90 days past due), the less they are worth, and the less likely they can be collected in full. If a big account is long overdue, you may try Small Claims Court or initiate other legal action. This can be a time-consuming process.

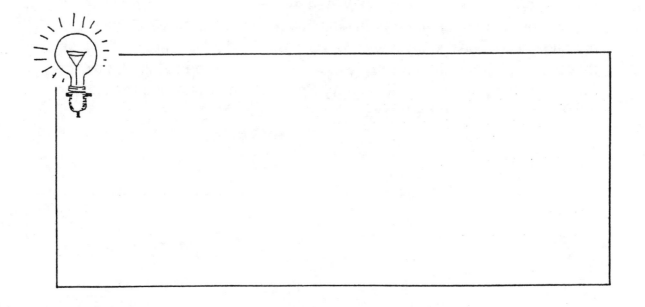

Tightening Up!

Inventory

The biggest concern here is to know for sure you're targeting your customers' needs. Ideally, you want to avoid tying up capital in excess stock while, at the same time, maintaining a balanced assortment of merchandise. Remember the 80/20 Rule of Thumb: 80% of your sales come from 20% of the normal product line.

For effective inventory control, you can either periodically count stock or count your daily sales. Whatever system you use, you're looking for up-to-date information at the least cost. To count sales, consider using a cash register tape, sales slips or a price ticket which is detached from the item when sold. Good stock records provide the information you need for reordering.

The key to inventory management is to know what and how much to order, when to order and what price to pay. When you add stock, make sure it's in affordable amounts, is of stable value and can be turned over reasonably quickly.

ONE IN EVERY FIVE FREIGHT BILLS CONTAINS AN OVERCHARGE!

Purchasing

Suppliers can vary tremendously. On the one hand, having one or a few major suppliers may qualify you for cumulative quantity discounts, special favors or valuable advice. On the other hand, having a wide variety of suppliers protects you by keeping your buying options open: you can shop around. Compare your suppliers frequently to be sure you're getting the best possible deal.

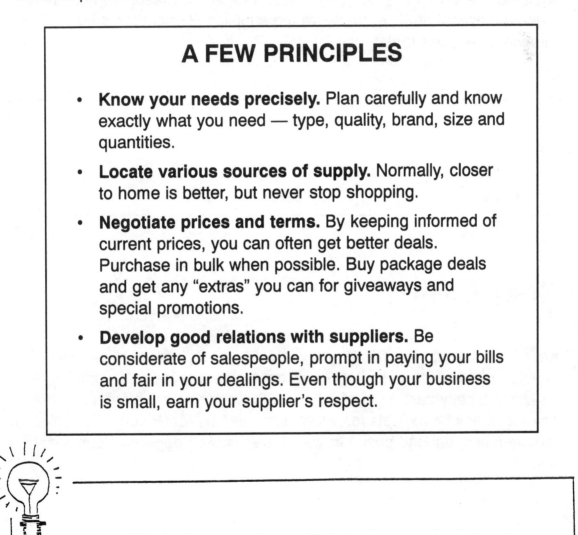

A FEW PRINCIPLES

- **Know your needs precisely.** Plan carefully and know exactly what you need — type, quality, brand, size and quantities.

- **Locate various sources of supply.** Normally, closer to home is better, but never stop shopping.

- **Negotiate prices and terms.** By keeping informed of current prices, you can often get better deals. Purchase in bulk when possible. Buy package deals and get any "extras" you can for giveaways and special promotions.

- **Develop good relations with suppliers.** Be considerate of salespeople, prompt in paying your bills and fair in your dealings. Even though your business is small, earn your supplier's respect.

ALWAYS GET THREE ESTIMATES ON LARGER PURCHASES!

Payables Policy

Know and utilize the terms your suppliers offer. Pay your bills at the best possible time — taking advantage of early payment discounts and avoiding interest on overdue payments. If for some reason you can't make a payment on time, forewarn the supplier. Remember, s/he's running a business too!

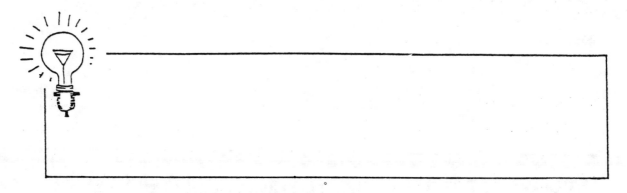

Petty Cash

Keep track of out-of-pocket payments which are too small to pay by check. Set a maximum limit for *cash* payments (maybe $10), and establish a petty cash fund of $20 to $50. Keep the money in a separate box together with receipts for every purchase made. Periodically replenish the amount spent and post it to your Expenditure Ledger for "business supplies."

Insurance

The purpose of an insurance program is to avoid exposing yourself to risks that might cripple your business. Although being in business is itself a risk, an alert entrepreneur will reduce the risks s/he bears directly.

Insurance coverage should be subject to hard-nosed analysis. Don't spend money needlessly. Periodically discuss with your agent or lawyer ways to reduce coverage and expenses.

WHAT IS ADEQUATE?

AT LEAST MINIMUM COVERAGE FOR:

	Yes	No
• Liability	☐	☐
• Fire insurance on building (if owned)	☐	☐
• Burglary and robbery	☐	☐
• Business Interruption	☐	☐
• Workmen's Compensation	☐	☐

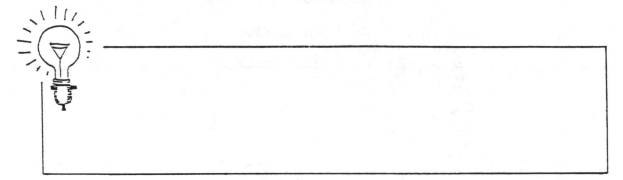

Bartering

Exchanging goods and services is often a way of cutting expenses. In these days when cash is in short supply, bartering can be an attractive way of doing business. It is wise to keep accurate and clear records of bartered transactions for your own control. At the end of the year, consult with your tax advisor about these transactions.

Energy

Some simple organizational changes could save you a lot of money in energy costs. Target your market more to the immediate geographic area. Consider ways of reorganizing routes and delivery schedules for greater fuel economy. Make your shop more energy efficient — insulating, weatherstripping, doors and partitions, etc.

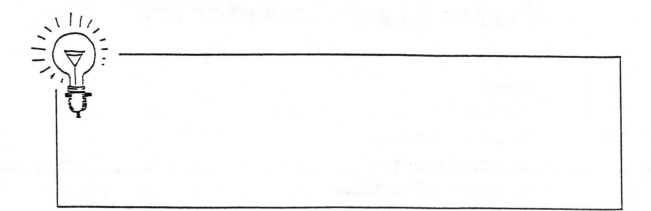

Plan for Better Financial Control

OVERALL OBJECTIVES (what you hope to achieve and the time frame)

_____

_____

_____

**COMPONENTS OF THE PLAN
(Which ones do you need?)**

	OBSERVATIONS & PRIORITIES

☐ OUTSIDE HELP
   ...Accountant
   ...Banker
   ...Other

☐ BASIC BOOKKEEPING SYSTEM
   ...Business Checkbook
   ...Review accounts breakdown
   ...One-write system

☐ CASH FLOW PROJECTION
   & ANALYSIS
   ...Three-month trial period
   ...Monthly analysis & reprojection

☐ BALANCE SHEET AND PROFIT
   & LOSS

☐ CREDIT POLICY & COLLECTING

☐ INVENTORY CONTROL

☐ PURCHASING PROCEDURES

☐ TAX MANAGEMENT & CONTROL

☐ OTHER:

   _____

   _____

   _____

NOW INCLUDE THIS IN YOUR YEARLY ACTIVITY PLAN!

STAY ON TOP OF THINGS!

We all know that hard economic times hit the "little guy" the hardest. This makes it particularly important for the micro business owner to cut costs, increase sales and control cash flow. To survive in today's economy, you just have to manage things better.

Your financial records will help you make decisions and meet your obligations. They will also help you know when you've reached your financial goals.

Section Four:

Capital
&
The Business Plan

IMPROVE YOUR CHANCES BY KEEPING
GOOD RECORDS AND PRESENTING YOURSELF WELL!

Your feelings and attitudes about money can get in the way
of a successful business. Attitudes about money are based on the
values we learned as children, on our life experiences and on the
culture and times in which we live. We've learned that money,
more than a mere medium of exchange, is often viewed as a
measure of a person's worth.

A WORD ABOUT MONEY....

There doesn't seem to be much "easy" or "cheap" money around these days. If it's true you "need money to get money," the dilemma of the small-time operator is pretty serious.

If you're a recent start-up or are just thinking about going into business, be prepared to put a lot of effort and inventiveness into finding the resources you need. Don't expect to get help from others if your ideas are not complete and if you've not fully committed your own resources to the project. To get started, most businesspeople we know pull together all of their liquid assets, borrow against their fixed assets and dig up whatever they can from relatives and friends.

Many people think that money is the solution to their problems. Sure it helps, but when you don't have it, you tend to hustle more. In the long run, this can result in establishing a better base for your business.

Steps to Finding Capital

STEP I:

PUT YOURSELF IN YOUR BANKER'S SHOES

Familiarize yourself with what banks and other lenders expect. Understand your banker's point of view and appraise the deal from his/her perspective.

STEP II:

PRESENT YOUR IDEAS IN A WRITTEN PLAN

A formally prepared Business Plan greatly improves your chances. Put it together in a way that's convincing and makes sense.

STEP III:

LOOK AT A COMPLETED BUSINESS PLAN

Here's how it goes together as a package. Evaluate the completeness of your ideas.

LENDERS AND INVESTORS EVALUATE THEIR CAPITAL COMMITMENTS CAREFULLY!

Step I:
Put Yourself
in Your Banker's Shoes

Working Capital

These days, you're in trouble if you look for long-term financing without adequate forethought and planning. Avoid problems by planning ahead! Carefully develop your expansion or modernization ideas by writing down the various requirements of your projects. This is the best way to analyze alternatives in an organized manner.

First, try cutting costs and streamlining your operation as a way of producing working capital. Then carefully analyze your situation before looking for outside capital. Are you managing well enough to be able to afford the cost of money? What are your possible sources of capital? Family? Friends? Suppliers? Bank? Do you have credit problems to resolve?

WANT TO ORGANIZE BETTER, INCREASE PROFITS, GET A LOAN? A WRITTEN BUSINESS PLAN IS ONE OF THE BEST WAYS WE KNOW TO ACCOMPLISH THESE GOALS!

Planning Ahead for Your Capital Needs

WHAT KIND OF FINANCIAL HELP WILL YOU NEED?

_____

_____

_____

_____

WILL YOU NEED TO BORROW MONEY? WHEN?

_____

_____

_____

_____

FROM WHOM WILL YOU BORROW?

_____

_____

_____

_____

ARE THERE ANY ALTERNATIVES TO BORROWING?

_____

_____

_____

_____

Choosing a Bank
...or a Banker

Before deciding on a bank, shop around. Every bank is different. Some are receptive to the needs of the small operator while others are more conservative. Some banks have a wider variety of services.

Find a bank (and a banker) that you feel comfortable with. Consider the bank's rates, services and the customer attention you can expect. Think about these points:

HOW BIG IS THE BANK AND WHAT ARE ITS POLICIES?
(Size big or small) may make a difference in services and credit availability. Does the bank have a reputation for lending to small businesses?

IS THE BANKER ALERT & PROGRESSIVE?
Does s/he understand the needs of a developing community and take an active part in community affairs?

IS THE BANKER FAVORABLY DISPOSED TOWARDS YOU?
How does s/he approach your problem? Does s/he appear interested and helpful?

WHAT ARE YOUR PROSPECTS FOR GETTING CREDIT?
Does the banker understand your particular needs? Is s/he prepared to service them?

Compare Banks

RATE EACH: (5) excellent
(4) very good
(3) good
(2) average
(1) poor

	BANK NAME				
Service Factors					
Customer Attention					
Small Business Philosophy					
Potential for Technical Assistance					
Potential for Credit					
Cost Factors					
Convenience & Location					
Banker's Friendliness					
TALLY					

NOTE:
This type of grid can be useful in making decisions. When comparing factors, however, be careful about giving them equal weight. Service factors are the most important. For example, a branch office that is convenient, but seldom has a loan officer on duty, is only open from 9 to 3 and has no night depository would have little to offer.

THE CHART ONLY POINTS YOU IN THE RIGHT DIRECTION!

What Banks Look For and Expect

Bankers want to make loans to business that are solvent, profitable and growing. They judge you (at least partly) on your farsightedness and your management. They expect you to plan ahead and anticipate your needs.

Try to understand your banker. Banks are profit-making operations — just as yours should be — and bankers have a big responsibility to shareholders and depositors alike.

One of the worst approaches is to appear at your banker's door and say, "Look, you gotta bail me out; my whole business is about to go under!" This tells the banker that you haven't stayed on top of things. Conscientious planning and management are essential if you want to use the bank's money. If you're in trouble, you'll need convincing evidence that your new plan will turn the business around.

A bank requires a lot of information on which to base its loan decisions. You'll have to supply much of it; the rest will come from credit files and outside sources.

CONSCIENTIOUS PLANNING AND MANAGEMENT ARE ESSENTIAL!

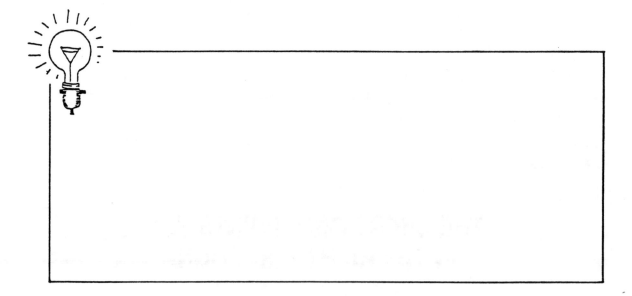

Your Rating as a Borrower
The Six "C"s of Credit

- **CHARACTER**
  What sort of a person are you? Are you trustworthy? Competent? Reliable? How good a manager are you? Will you squander funds?

- **CAPACITY**
  When and how do you plan to pay back the loan? Can the company generate enough to pay it back through its normal business activities? Does the Cash Flow Projection show this? Do past Profit & Loss Statements and Balance Sheets show this?

- **CAPITAL**
  What's the extent of your personal investment in the business? (If you're not a firm believer in your business, how can you expect the banker to be?)

- **COLLATERAL**
  Which of your assets could be used as security against a loan? Do you own real estate, stocks or bonds, vehicles and equipment, etc.?

- **CIRCUMSTANCES**
  What's the outlook for business in general and your business in particular? Does the loan make sense, or will it be the straw that breaks the camel's back?

- **COVERAGE**
  Do you have insurance against basic risks? How would the loan be repaid if there were an accident or catastrophe?

Why Some Banks Have a Hard Time Lending to Small Operators

- Due to lack of planning and cash management, most micro businesses approach the bank when it's already too late.

- The cost of processing a $5,000 loan is about the same as for a $50,000 loan, which leaves little incentive for spending time and effort on the smaller proposition.

- Banks like to see at least three years of accurate financial records and many micro businesses don't have these.

- Banks have difficulty financing new businesses without solid track records and they don't make speculative capital loans. (If you're looking for start-up capital, go elsewhere — to family and friends, a silent partner, a private investment company, etc.).

- Lending to one-person operations (most micro businesses) is risky. If you get sick or hurt, there may not be anyone to carry on the business.

- As a low-return, high-risk borrower, you have to have collateral to match the loan. Most micro businesses don't.

- Many small businesses are chronically under-capitalized from the beginning. You need capital to borrow capital.

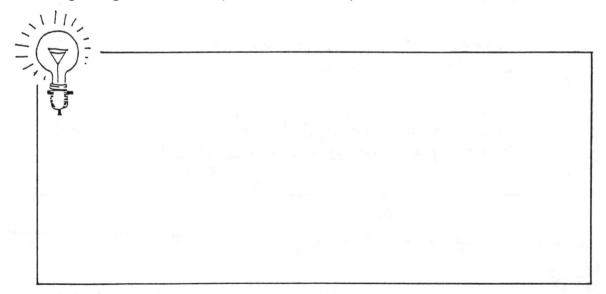

Preparing to Go to the Bank

Before approaching anyone for financing, determine how much capital is required, how much you'll put up yourself and whether the proposition is a reasonable one for the bank or investor. Then provide hard data to back up your proposition — Balance Sheet, Profit & Loss, Cash Flow Projection, etc.

YOU MAY BE ASKED:

- How did you use the money you started with?

- Is there a bigger market for you?

- Can you fill more orders if you get them?

- Can you stay ahead of the competition?

- Who says so besides you?

Bankers really want facts. They will carefully study your records, needs and plans. Since a great deal of confidential information is required, this is when good recordkeeping starts paying off.

Smart businesspeople use their records to create confidence on the part of potential lenders or investors. Your banker will be especially interested in evaluating your Profit & Loss Statement and Balance Sheet. The P & L shows how fast you're going while the Balance Sheet shows what you have to go on.

Approaching the Bank for a Loan

YOUR FIRST VISIT

Improve your chances by giving yourself enough lead time. Visit the bank(s) at least three months in advance of when you need money. This demonstrates foresight and allows you to say "I'm only here to see how the bank might be able to help me when I'm ready. Avoid going to the bank in a crisis situation.

For your own planning, ask about the types of loans available, the terms and conditions and the paperwork. Find out about short-term business loans and lines of credit as well as longer term loans. Show the banker your cash flow projections and get his/her opinion of them. What would s/he recommend to someone in your position? How serious a loan prospect are you for the bank?

TALK TO DIFFERENT BANKS AND COMPARE THEIR RESPONSES! (And don't neglect the local credit union.)

YOUR SECOND VISIT

You've decided what you need and you're now fully prepared to "talk turkey." This means you have a written business plan which clearly explains your situation and request. There's no better way to insure getting full consideration for your proposal.

Look at it from the banker's point of view. Which would you be more interested in: someone who shows up with a shoebox of old records and a vague idea of borrowing "some money," or someone who can show a written plan including an explanation of how much is needed, how the money will be used and how the loan will be repaid? Too many viable micro businesses get turned down at the banks due to inadequate information.

Again, talk to different banks about your proposal. A friend of ours took his proposal to five banks before accepting an exceptionally good rate from one.

OH NO! NOT ANOTHER SHOEBOX!!?

LOANS

Tim Sample

Types of Loans

SHORT-TERM LOANS are usually sought for working capital purposes, e.g., to built up inventory for a seasonal increase in sales. The repayment of such a loan may vary from 30 days to six months, and is expected when the purposes of the loan have been served. If your credit rating is good, you may get the money on an unsecured basis. Otherwise you'll have to put up collateral. Don't ask for a 30-day loan if you don't expect to have the funds in 30 days. A 30-day note that requires five renewals could be your last bank loan.

A LINE OF CREDIT is an understanding whereby the bank agrees to provide loans when needed up to a maximum preestablished limit. These loans, which may or may not be secured, are granted almost automatically during the period of the agreement (normally one year). A line of credit can be valuable in allowing the small operator to take advantage of unique opportunities. A line of credit must be paid up for at least 30 continuous days sometime during the one-year business cycle.

INTERMEDIATE TERM LOANS (commonly called Term Loans) are used for other than temporary needs. Such a loan gives you a chance to build equity. Typically, it is used to purchase an existing business or to help establish a new one. The money is normally paid back in installments. While a term loan is in force, you may be restricted in how you manage your business.

REGARDING TERMS...
Sometimes a lender may "give" a little on the terms if you negotiate. This is one reason for knowing what you can get from other banks. Try to get terms that you know your company can live with. Once they're set, you're stuck with them.

Be Fair and Reciprocate

Once you have a satisfactory banking relationship, continue to consult with your banker. Keep him/her informed about new developments in your business, discuss your financial problems and supply regular and complete financial statements — even at times when you have no need for credit.

If a bank helps you out with credit, reciprocate by opening a savings account and keeping your deposits there. Give them business. Spread the good word to friends and other serious-minded businesspeople in your community.

HAVING BANK CREDIT MAY BE HELPFUL AT SOME POINT. GET TO KNOW YOUR BANKER BEFORE THERE'S AN URGENT NEED!

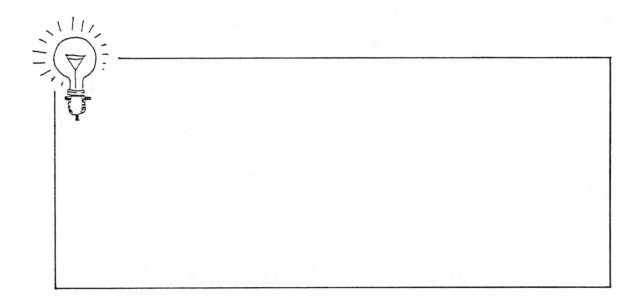

STAY ON THE RIGHT COURSE!

Step II:

Present Your Ideas
in a Written Plan

The Formal Business Plan

A WRITTEN PLAN HELPS YOU

- **MANAGE THE BUSINESS**
  By carefully thinking things out, you pinpoint problems, correct organizational and production errors and manage more efficiently.

- **EXPRESS YOURSELF CONVINCINGLY & CONCISELY**
  Writing things down helps you to organize and consolidate your ideas so that you are more effective in selling yourself and your business.

- **PREPARE PROMOTIONAL MATERIALS**
  Having a written plan will save you time and effort when it comes to putting together brochures and other printed materials.

- **USE OUTSIDE HELP EFFICIENTLY**
  Since the plan is a basis for presenting your ideas and getting input from others — your accountant, a business consultant, prospective suppliers, etc. — it will provide more complete information which could save time in the long run.

- **STRUCTURE A LOAN REQUEST OR ATTRACT INVESTORS**
  It puts your best foot forward and demonstrates that you're a serious manager with lots of good ideas and the know-how to make something work.

In this section, we guide you in putting together a formal, written business plan. Such a plan includes a brief narrative description of your business plus a series of annexes with financial information to support your proposal or request to bankers and investors. To help you in the process, we've included lots of examples from already completed business plans.

We remind you that lots of forethought and planning goes into effective management work. It does take time and there are rewards. It's said that every hour spent in planning saves you at least four hours later on. Anything you do to plan is better than a shot in the dark. By stepping back from your company's daily operation to review developments and possibilities more objectively, you may begin seeing things in a different light.

The plan outlined here is suitable for use as an in-house organizational tool or for presenting your business ideas to others.

NARRATIVE DESCRIPTION

A maximum of three to four neatly typed pages including

STATEMENT OF PURPOSE

BUSINESS DESCRIPTION

MARKET

MANAGEMENT

PRODUCTION & PERSONNEL

A Few Examples
of the Statement of Purpose

Our goal is to operate a more efficient and profitable business to provide both management and personnel a safe, happy and clean working environment in which to produce a quality product in a timely manner at a reasonable price, thereby promoting a good image for our company. This will encourage our customers to return.

A Printer

My long term business objective is to provide a dependable, high quality welding service in the Onset area and expand enough to support my family well. ACME Welding Service is presently seeking a capital improvement loan of $5,300 and a line of credit of up to $10,000. The $5,300 will finance the renovation of my shop facilities and the line of credit will be used as needed to offset cash flow problems during the coming year. Renovation of the shop will allow me to operate full-time during the winter months and make working conditions safer.

A Welder

...to organize business better so that it runs more efficiently and produces higher profits. So I know where the money is going and can plan ahead for slack times! So the management end of the business isn't neglected and new ideas don't fall to the wayside for lack of communication!

A Chimney Sweep

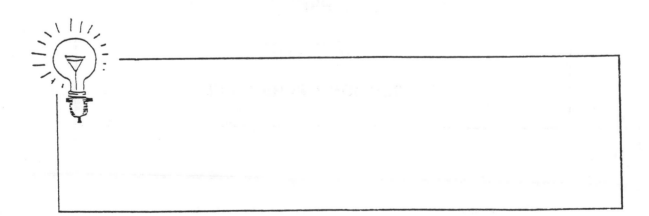

STATEMENT OF PURPOSE

Why do you want a business plan? Prepare a short description. It may simply state that you want to organize your business better so that it runs more efficiently and produces higher profits. It may also briefly state your plans for expansion or consolidation, including what you need to put them into action — credit, manpower, equipment, etc.

A Few Examples
of the Business Description

The Goose Eyed Shuttle is a textile arts business whose primary focus is in the handwoven production of rugs and the production of written research in the areas of textiles. High pile rag rugs, uniquely designed, are the main product; shawls, wall hangings, tapestries, and decorative usable items for the home are also produced in limited amounts. Classes and workshops in weaving, drafting and design, and special weaving techniques are given every other year.

A Weaver

This is a welding service organized as a sole proprietorship with no outside employees. Customers from two counties bring objects to my shop in Onset to be repaired and welded, or I use my portable equipment to do the work on location. Currently I am able to weld full-time only nine months of the year, but renovations of the barn will allow me to bring large projects inside during the winter. Almost any type of broken metal can be repaired and welded at my shop.

A Welder

A. B. Letterman, Inc. is a 50-year-old business, which operates as a Sub-Section S corporation. We are located at 500 Grant St. at the very edge of downtown Lincoln. We are primarily a letterpress and offset print shop but we also manufacture rubber stamps and do plastic laminating. We have eight direct competitors for printing and rubber stamps, as well as a number on the periphery of our trading area. We have no competition in our plastic laminating.

The Printer

This should briefly describe the central activities of your business. Be sure to mention the type of business, its organization, its location, the major products and services, any unique features (how it differs from the competition).

A Few Examples of the Market Write-Up

My rugs are marketed mainly in summer tourist shops in Maine, at craft fairs, and by orders from personal contact with buyers. I am in the process of developing sales representatives in New England and the San Francisco Bay Area.

The Weaver

Presently the bulk of our market is wholesale through fine craft and furniture stores. Our work is sought out by people in the medium to higher income ranges who want quality products and are willing to spend time and money for what they want. We offer a broad range of products and also build to specification. The growth potential of our market is not limited to our area, or even to Maine. We are now advertising regularly in local and statewide newspapers. Our new brochure is designed so that it can be updated regularly. New signs are being made for our building and our truck. Maine has a fast growing population of professional people bringing more and more demand for our services and products.

The Furniture Maker

I am the only certified welder in the area with complete (all metals) service available both in-shop and on the road. The growth potential for my company is tremendous since the only real competition comes from the person who does his metal working himself. Presently, my customers include local farmers, truckers, loggers, campers, boaters, and even housewives. Anyone with a piece of machinery or fabricated metal could need a qualified welder at some point.

The Welder

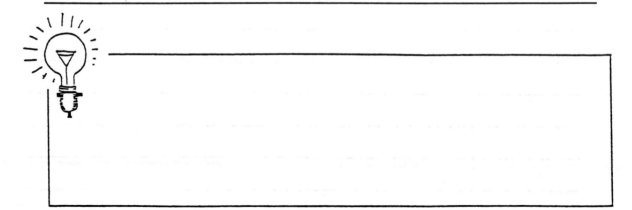

A good deal of thought must go into defining your market. Accurate "target marketing" may be the difference between a business that fails and one that flourishes. Describe your market precisely. How big is it? What portion of it will be yours? Identify the competition and appraise your market potential.

A Few Examples
of the Management Write-Up

Except for three hours a week spent on bookkeeping, I spend all my time in production and service. I have spent my life fixing all kinds of machinery and have worked steadily in the metal business for the past eight years. I also have management experience running a boat dealership that will help me to make this business a success. At this time, I receive assistance from a general business service and from ABCO for technical information on welding.

The Welder

I use a cash flow projection and a monthly bookkeeping system to organize and plan business activities. The Goose Eyed Shuttle has both checking and savings accounts, a large inventory of equipment, and has been able to maintain its original rule of never letting expenses be over the amount of money available from business revenues or the resources of the owner.

The Weaver

I spend most of my time on product development, production and promotion. My wife is responsible for bookkeeping and office management. We retain the help of a professional bookkeeper in addition to a general business service. I managed my own carpentry business in Boston prior to coming to Maine, and have always been keenly interested in building a successful business. I completed two years of machinist training after high school. Since childhood I have worked with wood and have a long-standing reputation for creativeness and attention to detail. I work well with others and have good directive abilities.

The Furniture Maker

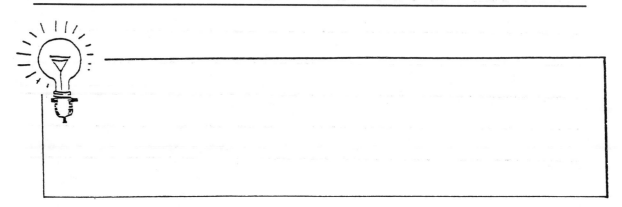

MANAGEMENT

Include a thorough review of your abilities and use of resources — particular experiences or skills you have that enable you to run the business well. List anyone who helps you manage better — accountant, lawyer, etc. Describe procedures that demonstrate you are managing the business: cash flow analysis, regular business meetings, yearly review, use of outside resources, etc.

A Few Examples
of the Production Write-Up

As an older business, we have many established accounts. We recently moved into larger facilities and have initiated changes in production with the ultimate goal of increasing sales. We organized a "Chain of Command" and appointed a shop foreman. This, and a series of other measures, gives me more time to plan and manage. We have over two dozen suppliers, 12 of which are major. Our equipment includes five presses, 2 cutters, 2 typesetters, and a complete darkroom. We also have everything needed to laminate, to manufacture stamps and to make 20" x 40" magnetic signs. There are four full-time and two part-time employees, who, with our new organizational chart, are working at peak efficiency. Our people work together well as a team.

The Printer

First an appointment is made, relevant information gathered and an estimate is given. If I'm way off in my quote, Lucky will re-quote it before beginning work.

The basic procedure is:
   (1) Arrive at household, evaluate the heating situation, decide what equipment is to be used (brushes, scrapers, vacuum, etc.)
   (2) Tape outlets to prevent any uncontrolled soot!
   (3) Brush/scrape chimney clean, clean out stove pipes and bottom of chimney.
   (4) Re-install stove pipes/stove.
   (5) Advise as to any corrections to improve heating efficiency and safety.

We eventually want our own facilities so there can be a separate office, and a shop for chimney care products!

The Chimney Sweep

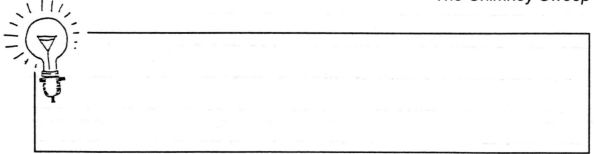

PRODUCTION & PERSONNEL

Write a few words about basic business operations. How does your business work and who makes it run? Include something about supplies and suppliers, the equipment used and your facilities. Describe your workforce and any major functional breakdowns.

The Annexes to the business plan say something important about the financial status of your business and your personal situation!

ARE YOU RUNNING YOUR BUSINESS... OR IS YOUR BUSINESS RUNNING YOU?

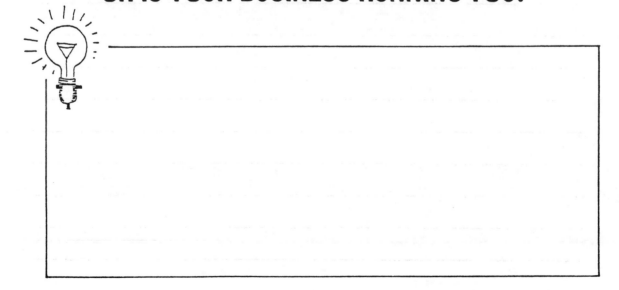

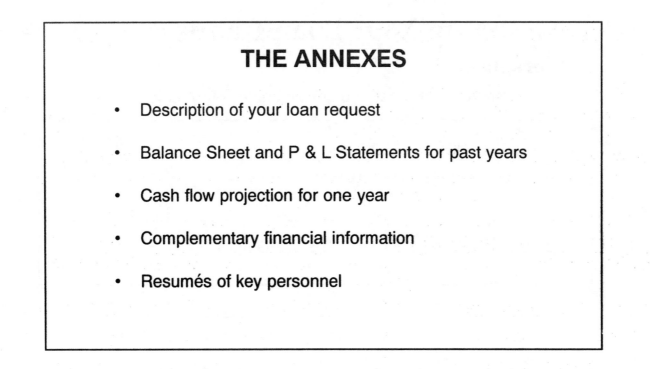

THE ANNEXES

- Description of your loan request

- Balance Sheet and P & L Statements for past years

- Cash flow projection for one year

- Complementary financial information

- Resumés of key personnel

Most bankers agree that if the business is three years old, it should provide three years' P & L figures. In addition, a graph or chart showing monthly trends is useful when applying for a loan.

The trends and the track record are big factors. Ideally, you should show how your business has had steady growth. If not, maybe you can point out your mistakes and demonstrate how they were recognized and corrected.

TRY TO ANTICIPATE THE BANKER'S QUESTIONS!

Developing Your Loan Request
A Worksheet

Use this worksheet to organize and clarify your ideas.

---

(1) THE AMOUNT NEEDED: _____

(2) TYPE OF LOAN SOUGHT:

_____

(3) WHAT THE MONEY WILL BE USED FOR:

_____

_____

_____

(4) OTHER RESOURCES & HOW THEY ARE TO BE USED:

_____

_____

_____

(5) EXPECTED IMPACT OF THE LOAN ON THE BUSINESS:

_____

_____

_____

(6) HOW MONEY WILL BE GENERATED TO REPAY THE
LOAN:

_____

_____

_____

(7) COLLATERAL OFFERED AS SECURITY:

_____

_____

Complementary Financial Information
Another Worksheet

By organizing this information in one place, you'll be able to quickly transfer it to any standardized forms required by the lending institution.

OUTSTANDING LOANS & FINANCIAL COMMITMENTS

Creditors Name, Address & Account Number	Purpose	Total Amt.	Unpaid Bal.

Today's Date:_____

CREDIT REFERENCES
(Names and addresses of other institutions and suppliers)

_____

_____

_____

_____

_____

CHECKING & SAVINGS ACCOUNTS
(Names and addresses of institutions and account numbers)

_____

_____

_____

_____

OTHER ASSETS
(Stocks and bonds, real estate owned, etc.)

_____

_____

_____

CHARACTER REFERENCES
(Anyone who can speak about you from a professional point of view.)

_____

_____

_____

_____

_____

ACCOUNTANT
(Name, address & phone)

LAWYER
(Name, address & phone)

When you're not using a standardized form, you may want to include a release such as this in your cover letter:

For the purpose of procuring credit from time to time, I furnish the foregoing as a true and accurate statement of my financial condition. Authorization is hereby given to the bank to verify in any manner it deems appropriate any and all items indicated in this application.

_____   _____
Date   Signature

_____   _____
                                Position or Title

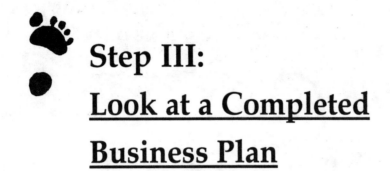

Step III:

<u>Look at a Completed</u>
<u>Business Plan</u>

This plan for Smith's DownHome combines elements from several real business plans developed by our clients. Remember, your objective is to concisely present your ideas and to put your best foot forward.

ALWAYS PUT YOUR BEST FOOT FORWARD!

BUSINESS PLAN
and
FINANCIAL PROPOSAL

for

SMITH'S DOWNHOME
PRODUCTS & SERVICES

OWNERS:

**Joe & Helen Smith
P.O. Box 777
Smalltown, Maine
Tel.: 555-5555**

FEBRUARY, 19____

STATEMENT OF PURPOSE

The purpose of this plan is to organize the business better so that it produces higher profits and functions more efficiently. **Smith's DownHome** is currently seeking a short-term loan of $8,000 to build inventory for its upcoming busy season. The business has experienced steady growth since its inception in 1980 and expects to gross over $60,000 this year.

BUSINESS DESCRIPTION

Smith's DownHome is a sole proprietorship based in Smalltown, Maine. Ours is principally a home renovation business. We sell and install a wide variety of products including major kitchen appliances, floor coverings, countertops, paneling, etc. We are equipped to handle most any type of home remodeling job, and pride ourselves on the quality of our products and service. Our customer attention includes on-site advice on interior design and modifications — a unique service that we alone offer.

Our business is located in our home which is within a half-hour drive from either Anywhereville or Anothertown. We modified two rooms to provide us with ample space for a display and sales area, and parking is readily available in front.

MARKET

Our market is primarily within a 25-mile radius of Smalltown. Over the past four years, we have developed a good core of steady customers who come to us because of our convenient location, the quality of our products and service and our fair prices. Since 1980, a large part of our business has come through referrals, and approximately one-third of our clientele are steady customers. Except for a short seasonal slump in the middle of the winter, we maintain a steady flow of business throughout the year.

We do both sub-contract work for full-time builders and our own private installations. The sub-contracts account for about 40% of our work, but the private installations give us a higher profit margin and a steady income.

Our competition in the immediate area is from two larger building supply companies located in Anywhereville and Anothertown. Neither of these competitors cuts significantly into our market due to our efficiency, superb customer attention and the full range of services we offer. Our prices are fair and we have a good reputation for standing behind our products and work. This, together with our year-round advertising, explains the continuous increase in monthly sales that we have experienced since last spring (about 10% per month).

We already have several jobs lined up for this spring (two larger contracts and five private installations). Prospects for this summer and fall are very promising, especially if the current building trends continue. We think we can project a modest expansion of our inventory to help us capture a larger share of the market. We are anxious to move more aggressively in our own installation and remodeling work where there is a higher profit margin. To do this, we have developed a comprehensive marketing strategy which includes advertising, special mailings and direct contact with certain targeted customers.

PRODUCTION

Our operation is entirely oriented towards meeting customer needs and offering the best possible value for the money. The products we sell are not the most expensive nor the cheapest, but those that will serve the customer's specific needs best.

To keep prices down, we are careful to diversify suppliers. Our products come from a wide variety of sources, and we routinely shop around to keep our channels of supply open and diversified.

To the extent possible, we group our jobs according to location to save travel time and increase productivity. Joe and his assistant do all the installation and remodeling work while Helen takes care of the store traffic and telephone.

MANAGEMENT

We hold weekly meetings to determine where the business stands financially and to plan the week's activities. Helen does the bookkeeping on a daily basis. Last September, the bookkeeping system was completely reorganized; the company now uses a One-Write System and works closely with an accountant to keep the management function under close control.

The management of our company is especially enhanced by Joe's specific sales and technical experience. He managed W. W. Small Hardware in Onset for five years prior to becoming the branch manager of Crocker and Zowie in Anothertown. Just before starting **Smith's DownHome,** he worked for three years as installation and sales specialist with Norway Lumber in Anywhereville. Joe has participate in sales and marketing clinics offered by Frigidaire, Galaxie Carpets and others around the country, as well as many in-store training programs on sales and management.

Complementing Joe's more technical background, Helen grew up in a small business family where she learned the fundamental concepts of marketing, sales and finance. She took an accounting course recently and has also attended a variety of small business management seminars.

It is possible for micro businesspeople to organize their activities and fully develop their ideas. Carefully consider where you are and where you're going before asking others to join you on the path.

Before approaching a bank or anyone else for assistance, think about your plans and ask yourself some tough questions. "Do I really need credit?" "Will the loan generate enough income to justify the cost and the hassle?" View it as objectively as possible and put yourself in your banker's shoes. No banker wants to make a loan that will put a small company out of business.

Planning is important before and after receiving a loan, to assure that the money is used effectively, according to your written business plan. This is the best way to keep your business healthy and growing.

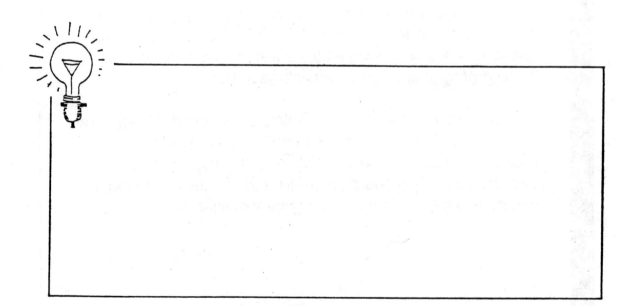

Section Five:

Time
&
Personnel

MATCH THE RIGHT PERSON TO THE RIGHT JOB!

Most small businesses begin as single-person operations — which frequently leads to a "do-it-yourself," "only I can do it right" mentality. This may be OK in the beginning, but most businesspeople quickly recognize the need for assistance.

Like all other aspects of business, your help must be managed, i.e., planned for, organized, directed and periodically evaluated.

Before hiring, be clear about your objectives for the business and be certain that you're using already existing resources to their fullest advantage. Take time to do a step-by-step business review. Make plans and carefully monitor your cash flow. Once you know where your business stands, and what you want to achieve in the future, it will be easier to manage your own time and to deal with others who are involved.

Hiring someone is a big responsibility. The close personal relationships that often develop in micro businesses are not found in larger companies. Hiring an employee can be like adopting a child. You may be able to purchase someone's time and labor, but loyalty, cooperation and enthusiasm must be carefully nurtured.

Learn to distribute the load and encourage others to take responsibility and to think for themselves. Motivate them! Encourage them to identify with and be a part of your business undertaking.

Steps to Managing Time & Personnel

STEP I:

PUT TOGETHER AN ORGANIZATIONAL CHART

This shows how the different jobs interrelate and helps you to not overlook important tasks.

STEP II:

ANALYZE TIME USAGE & WRITE JOB DESCRIPTIONS

If you are to focus on priority tasks that increase profits and improve your success, efficient time use is vital.

STEP III:

WEIGH THE PROS & CONS OF HIRING

Any way you cut it, the decision to hire employees is a big one with many ramifications.

STEP IV:

CAREFULLY SCREEN CANDIDATES BEFORE DECIDING

Be sure to hire the right person for the job!

STEP V:

OUTLINE BENEFITS & STRUCTURE COMMUNICATION

Once on board, encourage your employees to participate as full members of the team.

Are You Covering All the Bases?

The management process touches every aspect of your business. Careful time and personnel management go hand in hand as the company grows, and together will improve the efficiency of operations. It's necessary to take a close look at every aspect of the business and ask yourself...

ARE THE IMPORTANT JOBS GETTING DONE?

> Every job slot has to make good business sense; each new project must be measured for its cost-effectiveness.

WHO ARE THE MEMBERS OF MY TEAM?

> More people than you realize may be involved. Keep in mind that "outside" help such as your accountant, banker, vendors and customers all help you keep things going.

WHO DOES WHAT?
ARE WE USING TIME EFFICIENTLY?

> Clearly defined lines of communication and areas of responsibility are vital. People are more efficient when they work in areas of interest and strength.

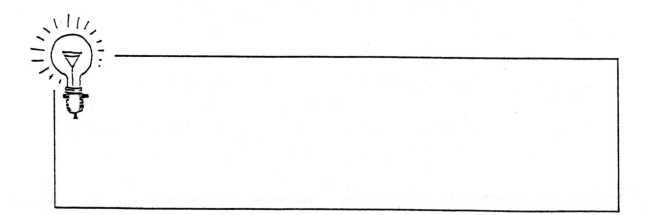

Step I:

Put Together
an Organizational Chart

Who Does the Work Around Here?

Indicate amount of time spent per week (or month) by you and each helper. Use a rough estimate of the number of hours or the percentage of time spent in each activity.

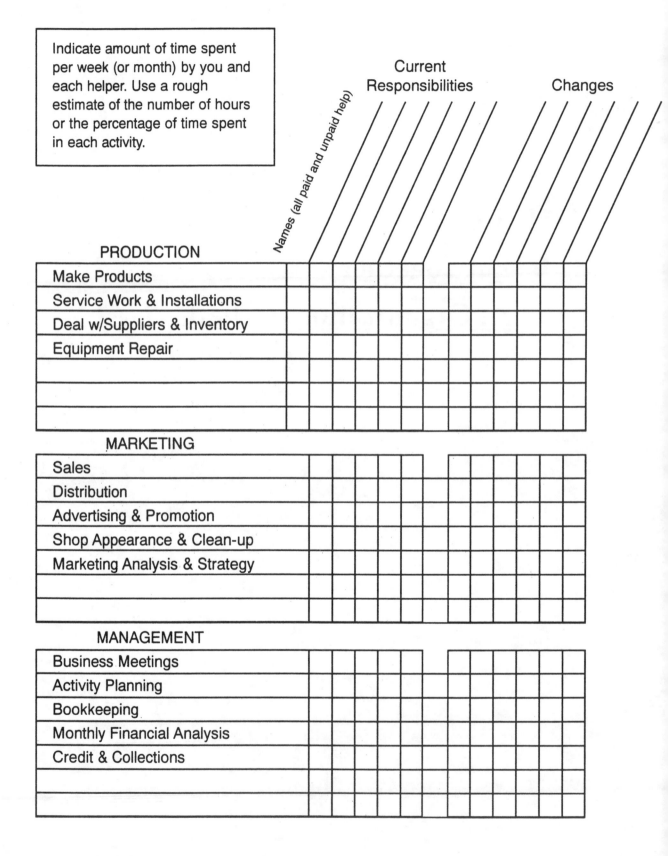

Names (all paid and unpaid help)

Current Responsibilities   Changes

PRODUCTION

Make Products											
Service Work & Installations											
Deal w/Suppliers & Inventory											
Equipment Repair											

MARKETING

Sales											
Distribution											
Advertising & Promotion											
Shop Appearance & Clean-up											
Marketing Analysis & Strategy											

MANAGEMENT

Business Meetings											
Activity Planning											
Bookkeeping											
Monthly Financial Analysis											
Credit & Collections											

The Organizational Chart

Many individual tasks/jobs fit together to make a business run. Though performed separately, all are needed, and the people doing them need to communicate and be incorporated into the overall operation.

An Organizational Chart is a visual representation of how different jobs fit together in a business. It helps you make sure you're covering all the bases. It helps you understand and relate to your business better. It shows who is (or is not) working in his or her areas of strength.

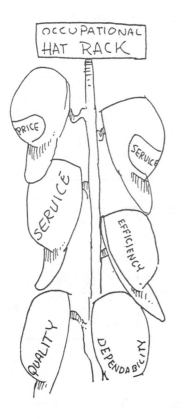

THE HATS THAT MUST BE WORN

General manager, sales person, marketing manager, shipping & receiving clerk, advertising manager, secretary & customer relations person, promotion copywriter, file clerk, production manager, graphic artist & printer liaison, production worker, bookkeeper, accountant.

If working with a spouse or in a partnership, be realistic about the roles each person plays. Less "active" partners often wind up doing administrative or book work that can strain a relationship — especially when it wasn't planned that way.

Most self-employed people are sole proprietors. Other micro businesses may be partnerships, cooperatives or corporations. The organizational chart you draw for your business will vary somewhat according to the legal structure. A typical sole proprietorship will look something like this:

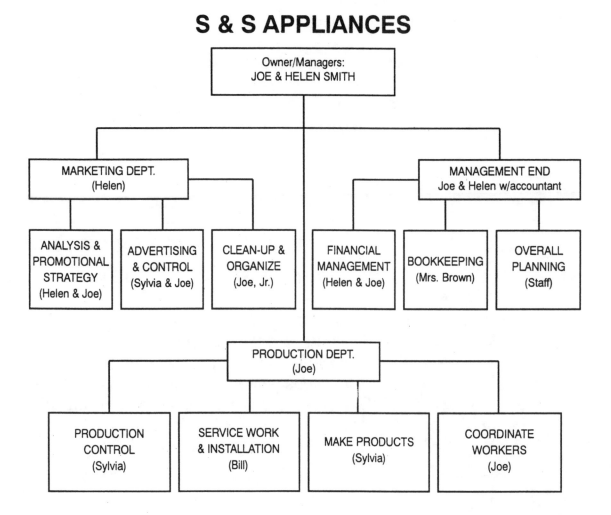

S & S APPLIANCES

Owner/Managers:
JOE & HELEN SMITH

MARKETING DEPT.
(Helen)

MANAGEMENT END
Joe & Helen w/accountant

ANALYSIS & PROMOTIONAL STRATEGY (Helen & Joe)

ADVERTISING & CONTROL (Sylvia & Joe)

CLEAN-UP & ORGANIZE (Joe, Jr.)

FINANCIAL MANAGEMENT (Helen & Joe)

BOOKKEEPING (Mrs. Brown)

OVERALL PLANNING (Staff)

PRODUCTION DEPT.
(Joe)

PRODUCTION CONTROL (Sylvia)

SERVICE WORK & INSTALLATION (Bill)

MAKE PRODUCTS (Sylvia)

COORDINATE WORKERS (Joe)

Note that this sole proprietorship is run by a husband/wife team. They have an accountant, a bookkeeper and two full-time employees. Their son is in charge of cleaning up the shop. The business is broken down into three major areas of activity — marketing, administration and production. Each is subdivided into more specific tasks, and these in turn could be further subdivided (which is where job descriptions come in). Note how someone is assigned to and responsible for each activity.

Draw an organizational chart for your business. Design it so that all the important bases are covered. Make sure responsibilities are clearly defined.

---

(1) Fill in the major areas of endeavor — production, marketing, etc.
(2) Divide "Departments" into their components.
(3) Designate areas of responsibility.
(4) Circle the problem areas and consider possible changes.

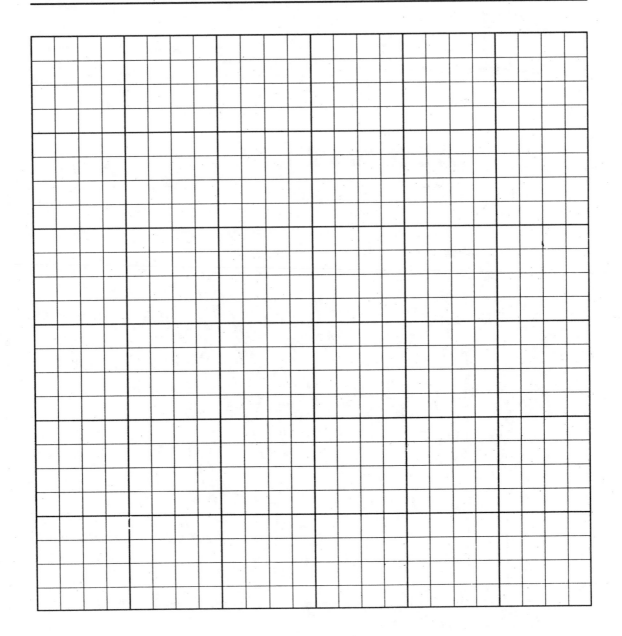

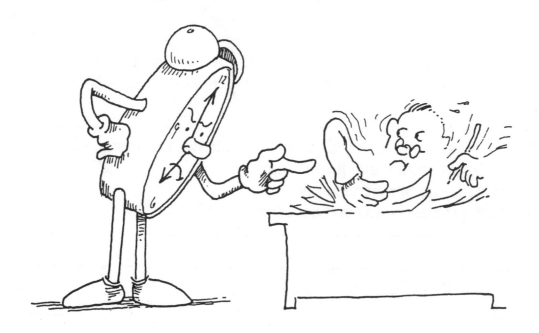

WHO'S IN CHARGE HERE?

Step II:

Analyze Time Usage

&

Write Job Descriptions

Time Management
A Few Principles

Because there are so many things to do and so few people to do them, time management is vital to the micro businessperson. Your attitude toward time and its wise use is a key consideration. You can accomplish the important things if you decide what they are and set priorities. By examining time wasters, you can find ways of dealing with obvious drains on your available time.

BETTER TIME MANAGEMENT

- Focuses your activities.

- Helps things run smoothly to get essential jobs done.

- Enriches the work and opens up time for the things you like.

- Improves the quality of time spent with others.

When important matters are taken care of expeditiously, everyone's time (your own, employees', customers', vendors') is used to the best advantage. You may be able to reduce your working hours and have more time for family, friends and self. Your outlook on the business will be brighter, and you'll be better able to plan for the future.

The first step toward improved time use is developing a positive attitude toward it. Don't let time control you. Time management is a learned skill.

The way you use time affects everyone else's use of it. When time wasters strike, they steal your productivity and profits. Learn to identify the time robbers — whatever and whomever they are. Eliminate the biggest offenders and regulate the others.

START WITH YOURSELF!

- How do I spend my time?
- What are my strengths and weaknesses as a manager?
- How much time do I spend "doing what I do best"?

HOW ABOUT EVERYONE ELSE?

- Is each person doing his/her job?
- Are there weak areas that need attention?
- Can we work together to redistribute responsibilities?

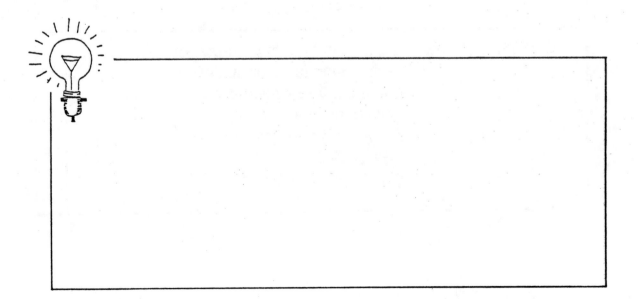

Time Wasters

DO THEY PLAGUE YOUR OPERATION IN...		A Little	Some	A Lot
PLANNING?	Unclear objectives			
	Trying to do too much			
	Haste or impatience			
	Shifting priorities			
	Unrealistic time estimates			
	Not listening to others			
ORGANIZING?	Cluttered workspace			
	Too much paperwork or communication			
	Inadequate equipment or facilities			
	Lack of internal systems			
	Duplicated effort			
	Poor distribution of responsibility			
DIRECTING?	Lack of teamwork			
	Too much attention to detail			
	Untrained employees			
	Indifference or lack of motivation			
	Procrastination or indecision			
	Not thinking things out, making snap decisions			
CONTROLLING?	Starting and not finishing tasks			
	Lack of standards or guidelines			
	Aural and visual distractions			
	Inadequate information			
	Drop-in or telephone socializing/ idle talk			
	Absenteeism or tardiness			

PLANNING

It takes time, but each hour spent planning may save four later on. It helps eliminate crisis management, which is inefficient. Don't go too many directions at once. Set priorities so there is time for essentials. Find satisfaction in doing important things. Give others an opportunity to contribute their ideas for the overall operation or aspects of it.

ORGANIZING

Set up basic systems for production, marketing and administration (especially for repetitious or routine work). Write job descriptions to clarify the division of responsibility. Consider improving equipment or facilities. Prepare "to do" lists in advance with A-B-C priorities. Organize desk areas for greater efficiency with file holders, stack trays, etc.

DIRECTING

The better the planning, the easier the directing. Decision-making should be done in light of overall goals. Keep communication channels open between you and your team members. When you procrastinate, it's usually due to a task which is overwhelming, unpleasant or not a priority.

CONTROLLING

Be clear about the rules and quality standards. Learn to say "no" graciously to those who might unduly waste your time or another's time. Keep a time log and find out about "Day-Timers" scheduling systems (One Day-Timer Plaza, Allentown, PA 18195).

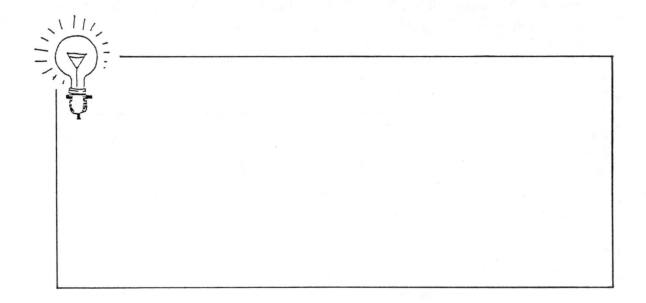

Time Tips

- Allow at least 1–2 hours a day of uncommitted time. Get the absolute "musts" out of the way early to feel less frantic about interruptions.

- A 50-minute work period followed by a 10-minute break gives optimal performance. Breaks let you assimilate information and replenish the brain's oxygen. You'll return to work refreshed and relaxed.

- Doing the same thing at the same time each day both conserves energy and cuts down on indecision. Pick a specific time each day/week to make phone calls, do paperwork, run errands.

- Develop systems for dealing with ongoing problems and repetitious tasks. Checklists help insure that nothing is left out.

- Control meeting time. Have a specific agenda of what you want to cover and specify the amount of time that will be spent on each item.

- Do the most profitable parts of large projects first. The sense of satisfaction you get from seeing immediate results will motivate you to complete the remainder.

- Getting started is the most difficult step for procrastinators, so start small. Break your project into parts and tackle them one at a time. Even if you devote only half an hour a day to your project, you'll see noticeable progress at the end of a week's time.

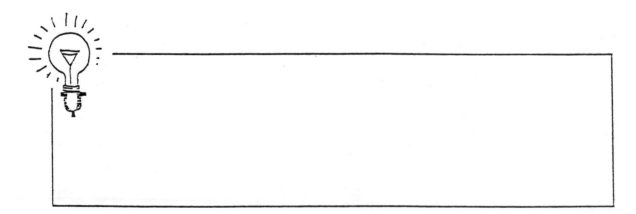

Acknowledgment: Many of the concepts on these two pages were adapted from *Update on Human Behavior*, Vol. 7 No. 1. Human Services, Inc., 5307 E. Mockingbird, Dallas, TX 75206.

The 80/20 Rule of Time Management

80% of your RESULTS come from...
20% of your EFFORTS!

When all items are arranged in order of value, 80% of the value comes from only 20%. Conversely, only 20% of the value comes from 80% of the items. Therefore, concentrate on higher-value tasks at the expense of lower-value tasks. Perfectionism is only worth approaching when 80% of the value comes from the *last* 20% of the effort.

75% of effective time management is eliminating the unimportant things that take up time without generating benefits.

There's a high burnout rate among small business people, so take care of yourself. Schedule vacations and time off well in advance to plan around them. Eat right. Get exercise. Slow down and breathe deeply when the going gets tough.

IT ONLY TAKES 21 DAYS TO MAKE A HABIT!

Job Descriptions

Simply stated, a job description is a written summary of facts about a particular job. It outlines duties, how they are to be performed, the skills needed and the importance of the job. It deals with the basic requirements of a job, **not** with how well an individual does it.

Just as a written plan sets a business on course, job descriptions outline what each person has to do to keep a business moving toward its goals. Job descriptions help you analyze the efficiency of your operation. They structure the communication between you and your employees, giving you both a better understanding of what's expected. They help you appraise whether additional help is needed or if responsibilities can be better distributed.

Know the vital work functions and have a good idea of each individual's strengths and weaknesses (starting with yourself). Match the best people to the best jobs for them, building on each person's strengths.

THINK JOBS THROUGH CAREFULLY!

- Ask your employees' opinions on how jobs can be done better.

- Have each list his/her job tasks and estimate the hours per week to complete each task.

- Carefully study each list, making observations and adding other functions you consider important.

By doing this, you and your employees will get a better idea of the relative priority to be placed on the different functions.

When establishing a new job, write the best description you can and let the employee test it. This way you can revise the description as necessary during the test period.

Job Description
A Worksheet

JOB TITLE: _____

Major Functions, Tasks, Responsibilities	Hrs/wk.	Qualifications Needed

Approved by: _____ Date: _____

SMITH'S DOWNHOME APPLIANCES
JOB DESCRIPTION
STORE MANAGER

(1.) Contribute to the creation of a working environment that supports the profitable, production-related goals of SMITH'S DOWNHOME APPLIANCES while enabling each person to reach his/her highest potential. Recommend changes and develop ideas for the improved operations of the company.

(2.) Work to establish a safe, responsible working environment.

(3.) Implement agreed upon work plans. Understand the specifics of projects to be undertaken, questioning the general manager and co-workers as appropriate.

(4.) Develop a basic plan of action for each workday, putting together a daily "to do" list. Assign A (vital), B (important), C (some importance) priorities to the list.

(5.) Answer the phone in a courteous, friendly manner. Take accurate messages.

(6.) Manage the Smalltown store:

    a. Open and close store using established procedures.
    b. Tend to customers and handle routine over-the-counter sales.
    c. Price merchandise following mark-up guidelines.
    d. Maintain an up-to-date inventory on all white and brown goods.

(7.) Be a responsible salesperson by thoroughly familiarizing yourself with all merchandise. Maintain the store appearance and promotional displays. Prepare *written* quotes for customers.

(8.) Keep the books and company records as required by the general manager and the company accountant. Be organized and neat in your work.

(9.) Maintain a positive attitude, fully participate as a team player and act in a friendly professional manner in interactions with customers, co-workers and managers.

    a. Respond to supervision positively.
    b. Bring problems promptly to the general manager's attention.
    c. Be flexible and open to change.
    d. Take responsibility for both giving and receiving complete communication.
    e. Help supervise and/or train others when requested to do so.

(10.) Maintain the confidentiality of proprietary company information.

(11.) Readily accept other reasonable duties and responsibilities.

I, _____ , have read this job description, fully understand the conditions set forth, and will perform my duties to the best of my ability.

DATE _____ SIGNATURE _____

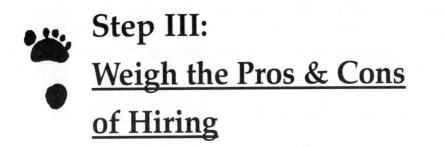

Step III:
Weigh the Pros & Cons of Hiring

Alternatives to Hiring

SUBCONTRACTORS

An alternative to hiring permanent employees is sometimes sub-contracting. Outside contractors are "people in business for themselves, who follow an independent trade and offer their services to the public." (I.R.S. definition). Be sure to hire only subcontractors who carry their own workmen's compensation and health insurance, otherwise you may be held liable should they be injured on the jobsite. Check references! By being careful to hire only honest, reputable businesspeople, you'll save money and headaches.

Make sure you're not calling employees "subcontractors" just to avoid making the required benefit payments. A subcontractor doesn't punch a clock. You might supply the raw materials, but be careful about tools and workspace. Get a written contract and check with a lawyer to be on the safe side.

CONSULTANTS

Any growing business can frequently use expert advice. Always select people who are truly interested in your business, and sympathetic to your needs as a micro business. There are times when you'll want to work closely with these consultants so be sure they are people you trust. Always **shop around** and check references.

As a rule, don't have consultants do work you can do yourself. Ask them to advise you on general matters and teach you to do things for yourself.

If you pay over $600 during one year to a consultant or subcontractor, you must file a #1099 Non-Employee Compensation Form with the I.R.S.

DO I HAVE . . .

	Yes	No
• an ACCOUNTANT I trust?	☐	☐
• a LAWYER I trust?	☐	☐
• an INSURANCE AGENT I trust?	☐	☐
• a BANKER I trust?	☐	☐
• a BUSINESS ADVISOR I trust?	☐	☐

TAKE TIME TO FIND THE RIGHT OUTSIDE HELP!

The Decision To Hire

Careful assessment of your situation points to the fact that you need more help. Since you're managing better, things are under control and you have a clear idea of where you want to go. Now you need "people power."

Hiring an employee is a big step for your company. Make sure that the new position fits into your overall long-term goals. Never hire a person without a good reason. Personnel costs are fixed and come with obligations and responsibilities. Hiring unwisely can be a costly mistake, both in time and money. Will the increased overhead justify itself in the long run? Is your company stable enough to support more people? Is your cash flow strong enough to take on additional risks. Carefully weigh the pros and cons of these questions.

THE PROS

- Lessens your workload by sharing responsibilities.

- Increases production, sales and profit potential.

- Brings new talent, fresh ideas and more energy.

THE CONS

- Means increased paperwork (about twice as much).

- Raises your overhead (provisions for insurance, etc.)

- Brings stricter government regulations and scrutiny:

    - Workman's compensation

    - Unemployment insurance

    - Prompt and regular payment of withholding taxes

CAN WE SUPPORT MORE PEOPLE?

A WEEKLY OR BI-WEEKLY BUSINESS MEETING IS A GREAT WAY TO FOCUS EVERYONE'S ENERGY ON THE PROBLEMS AT HAND!

Do's and Don'ts of Hiring

DO
carefully assess your needs and consider all the alternatives to full time help.

DON'T
rush into anything! Take enough time to study the options and to make the right decision.

DO
prepare a written job description to outline specific tasks, the skills needed and minimal standards of performance.

DON'T
be persuaded to relax your standards in order to fit someone in who doesn't really fill your needs.

DO
interview various people: have at least three qualified candidates to choose from.

DON'T
hire the first person who comes along without considering others.

DO
make sure your recordkeeping systems are set up properly before hiring.

DON'T
put it off until after you see if the person works out.

DO
be clear about what's expected of the new employee and use a three- to six-month trial period.

DON'T
expect people to figure things out for themselves or to do things exactly the way you do.

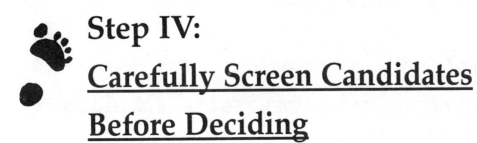

Step IV:
Carefully Screen Candidates Before Deciding

Where to Find People

LISTINGS of newspapers, magazines and trade associations.

REFERRALS of customers, suppliers, actual or former employees, organizations, etc.

SCHOOLS through student employment services and work-study programs.

GOVERNMENT on-the-job training programs.

VOCATIONAL REHABILITATION AGENCIES (special tax credits if you hire someone with a disability).

SMITH'S COOKWARE
Sales Positions Available
Full time/Part time
for someone who:

— is friendly and at ease with people.

— will enjoy learning about our products and will enjoy telling our customers about them.

— has an interest in food, food preparation, and cooking equipment.

— can take inventories.

— can write orders.

— is able to cheerfully work retail hours including evenings, Saturdays, Sundays, and holidays.

Previous sales experience desirable. Salary commensurate with experience. Send resume indicating position applying for to: Box 777, Smalltown, Interviews will be held the week of 10/1. No phone calls please.

How to Find Them

PRINTED JOB DESCRIPTIONS can be sent or given to employees, friends, customers, suppliers, clubs, churches, etc.

NEWSPAPER ADS, while effective, may leave you with the task of screening numerous applicants.

"HELP WANTED" SIGNS may work depending on the kind of help you seek but, rather than interviewing aspirants on the spot, have them fill out an application.

STATE EMPLOYMENT SERVICES can advise you about regulations, help you screen applicants, and tell you about special training programs or opportunities.

PRIVATE EMPLOYMENT AGENCIES do charge for their placement service, but are efficient and know their business.

SPREAD THE WORD-OF-MOUTH!

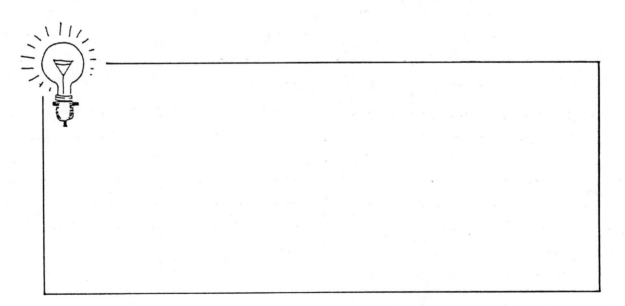

JOB APPLICATION

NAME: _____ TELEPHONE: _____

ADDRESS: _____

SCHOOLING

Elementary	From _____	to _____	
High School:	From _____	to _____	Where? _____
College:	From _____	to _____	Where? _____
Other (Please specify)	_____		

EMPLOYMENT

List below all present and past employment (including military) beginning with the most recent job. Use back of form if necessary.

Company Name & Address	From		To		Supervisor's Name	Reason For Leaving	Your Job(s)
	mo	yr	mo	yr			

May we contact these employers? Yes ☐ No ☐

Are you physically unable to perform certain kinds of work Yes ☐ No ☐

COMMENTS OR REMARKS

_____

_____

SIGNATURE: _____ DATE: _____

198

The Application Form

Since your objective is to find three qualified candidates from whom to choose, you'll probably "process" quite a few people. A good application form will help standardize the information you collect and allow you to compare people's backgrounds more easily.

An application form contains basic information about the applicant's professional, educational, and personal background. It also provides the names and addresses of previous supervisors so that you can check references. An alternative would be to ask people to supply you with resumés of their own design.

On the opposite page is a sample application form. Design your own or get one that's standardized from an office supply store. Ask each prospective employee to complete one.

THE APPLICATION HELPS YOU PICK WHO TO INTERVIEW AND GIVES YOU A WAY TO START THE INTERVIEW.

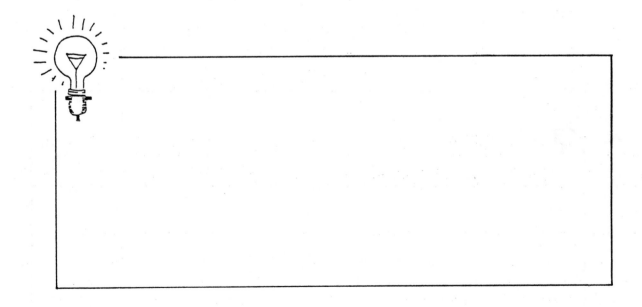

The Interview

The objective of an interview is to learn about the person's experience, work habits and skills. Encourage the applicant to talk about himself or herself. Do as little talking as possible yourself.

SPECIFIC QUESTIONS

- What did you do on your last job?
- What did you like or dislike about it?
- Which of your supervisors did you like best? Least?
- What's most important to you about a job?
- What are your career plans?

Carefully consider the answers given and look for clues to personality, habits, strengths and weaknesses. If you think you are interested in a particular applicant, ask him/her to check back with you later. Never commit yourself until you have interviewed all of the likely applicants. Allow a short break between interviews to jot down your impressions while they're fresh in your mind; also jot down any other questions you wish you'd asked. Keep good records of your thoughts or you may mix people up.

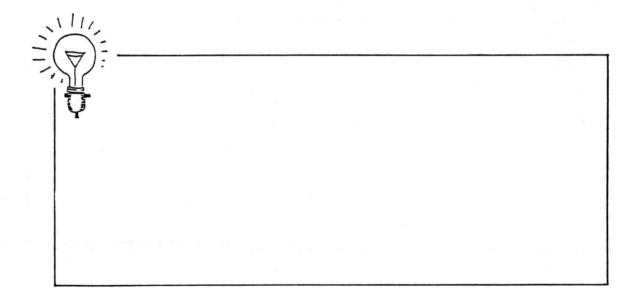

References

The only references worth checking are past supervisors' unless you happen to know someone who personally knows the applicant. It doesn't take much effort to check a reference, and you can gain useful information. Do it by phone. Mention the nature of your small business, and ask the former boss if s/he thinks this person would fit in.

ASK THE FORMER BOSS...

- Why did Joe leave?

- What are his strong and weak points?

- Would you re-hire him? For what position?

GET AT LEAST THREE GOOD CANDIDATES

Comparing the Applicants

Gather your information and carefully evaluate each person. Then compare your evaluations for the different candidates remembering the minimum qualifications for the job.

APPLICANT NAME:

_____

	Excellent	Very Good	Good	Average	Poor
Job Qualifications					
Stability of past employment					
Aspirations and expectations					
Self-motivation					
Need for employment					
Willingness to learn					
Ability to get along with others					
Growth potential					

REMEMBER EQUAL EMPLOYMENT OPPORTUNITY: "No one can be refused employment on the basis of race, nationality, sex or age."

GOT IT ALL TOGETHER NOW? YOU'VE RECRUITED WIDELY AND WISELY. YOU HAVE THREE GOOD CANDIDATES FOR THE JOB!

YOU'RE READY TO DECIDE!

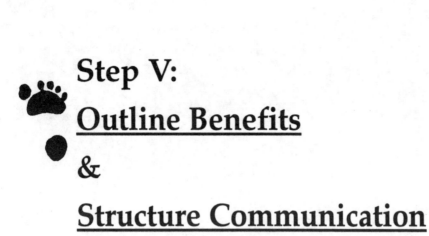

Step V:

Outline Benefits

&

Structure Communication

TO ACHIEVE YOUR GOALS
EVERYONE NEEDS TO WORK TOGETHER

Help your employees to feel at home. Introduce new people and explain how different jobs interrelate. Encourage questions. Share your plans for the company and ask for input. Learn to listen and keep the communication flowing.

Training

By providing training opportunities, you can reduce turnover, motivate your employees and build morale. Training gives everyone a chance to polish old skills and acquire new ones. It's an investment in the growth of your company.

Using job descriptions to guide you, determine training priorities. The specific type of training will depend on the job, the existing skills and the employee's interests and ambitions. Balance the cost of training against the cost of under-qualified or poorly motivated people. Look to the future.

ADULT EDUCATION COURSES often help people obtain new skills or knowledge valuable to the company.

SPECIAL CERTIFICATION COURSES in vocational training or other learning centers can help your small company grow and diversify.

ON-THE-JOB TRAINING PROGRAMS available through government agencies, can be a cost-efficient, organized method of getting extra help.

WORK-STUDY PROGRAMS through universities and secondary schools help both you and the student.

ENCOURAGE YOUR EMPLOYEES TO SHARE WHAT THEY'VE LEARNED!

HELP EACH OTHER TO LEARN!

Benefit Package

Think about the benefits you offer and prepare a short description of them. It will help set the tone for your operation and make people feel welcome, secure and fairly treated.

CONSIDERATIONS

WAGES
A salary or hourly rate based on fair, competitive scales. Any other economic incentives such as a percentage commission or bonus plan? How often will salaries be reviewed?

FRINGES
May include discounts on merchandise, paid additional training, life insurance, health insurance, etc. Trade associations sometimes offer group rates.

VACATIONS & HOLIDAYS
Largely depends on your size and budget. Which holidays? How much vacation will be given in the first year? Second year? Any special time when you prefer vacations to be taken?

TIME OFF
How do you treat emergencies and personal matters? Will the time off be deducted from the person's salary? What's your attitude toward longer leaves of absence?

TRAINING
What are the opportunities or requirements? Who will be responsible? Who will pay?

PROMOTION
What are the possibilities, if any? How about changes in title or responsibility?

Personnel Policy

Together with the benefit package, this helps you clarify a variety of issues while structuring the hiring process. It puts your company's internal procedures into a printed, usable form.

CONSIDERATIONS

HIRING
Some sort of fixed probationary or trial period is common practice and usually lasts from three to six months.

PERFORMANCE
Job descriptions help avoid misunderstandings and provide a base for evaluating performance. Will you routinely review performance? How often?

DISCIPLINE
Insubordination, repeated tardiness, poor quality work, sloppiness and personal appearance may all crop up and need to be dealt with.

GRIEVANCES
An opportunity to air grievances will give everyone a chance to express their feelings about the overall work situation.

SET THE RIGHT TONE!

EMPLOYEE POLICIES & BENEFITS

SMITH'S DOWNHOME APPLIANCES is an equal opportunity and affirmative action employer. All employees are covered under Social Security, Workmans' Compensation, and Unemployment Insurance.

BENEFITS

DAILY SCHEDULE & WORK BREAKS:
The workday is from 8:00 a.m. to 5:00 p.m., Monday through Friday, with a 10-minute coffee break at 10:00 a.m. Lunch is from noon to 1:00 p.m. on the employee's time.

PAID HOLIDAYS:
After the first year of employment, full-time employees will receive the following paid holidays: Memorial Day, Independence Day, Labor Day, Veteran's Day, Thanksgiving Day, Christmas Day, New Year's Day.

VACATIONS:
After one year of employment, employees receive 5 working days of paid vacation. After two years, employees receive 10 working days. Vacation time must be requested at least one month in advance and coordinated on the Central Calendar. Vacations are non-accumulative.

PERSONAL DAYS:
After one year with the company, employees receive four (4) paid personal days yearly for sickness or other necessities. Anyone taking a personal day must notify the manager as early as possible, and preferably give three days' advance notice.

SALARIES:
All new employees are subject to a three-month trial period after which their salary is reviewed. Thereafter, the salaries of all regular employees are reviewed during the month of January.

MERCHANDISE:
After six months with the company, full-time employees may purchase appliances and other merchandise, at cost, for their own personal use with the manager's approval.

EVALUATIONS:
New employees are evaluated every three months during the first year of employment. Thereafter, evaluations are conducted annually in the Spring. These evaluations are intended to structure communication and provide a vehicle for constructive criticism.

RESIGNATION:
To resign in good standing, an employee must give two weeks' written notice. This allows an employee to be paid for accumulated leave and any other accrued benefits.

LAYOFF:

If it is necessary to lay off an employee for any reason, 30 days notice shall be given *if at all possible.* Such employees may seek other employment during this time but only insofar as it does not unduly interfere with their work.

RULES & REGULATIONS

EMPLOYEES ARE EXPECTED

(1) to be cooperative, careful and respectful of others.

(2) to be prompt in reporting to work.

(3) to produce work that is neat and of high quality, and to keep their work places clean and free of debris or anything that may cause an accident.

(4) to care for and maintain company tools and equipment. This includes returning equipment, tools and materials to proper storage places as a consideration to others.

(5) to take the initiative of finding work (such as cleaning up, organizing equipment and materials, etc.) in the event of a lull in the day's planned activities.

(6) to opportunely bring any work-related problem to the attention of their immediate supervisor. This includes running low on supplies.

(7) to **not** use alcohol or illegal drugs on the job or prior to coming to work. Such use constitutes grounds for immediate dismissal.

**FAILURE TO COMPLY WITH THE ABOVE RULES MAY RESULT
IN A WRITTEN WARNING OR JOB TERMINATION**

BUSINESS MEETINGS

To discuss matters relevant to the operations of the company, monthly business meetings are held the first Wednesday of each month at 7:30 a.m. for no more than 45 minutes. Employees are expected to share their concerns and ideas for positive improvement at these meetings. The general manager is also pleased to meet individually with employees to discuss any problem.

I HAVE READ AND FULLY UNDERSTAND THIS POLICY.

Employee: _____ Employer: _____

Date: _____ Date: _____

Evaluating Performance

It's good practice to periodically evaluate employee performance —
maybe twice a year. Do it independently of salary reviews so that the
evaluation can be treated in the most positive, objective manner possible.

The goal is to find out how everyone is doing, to provide objective
feedback, and to keep employer–employee communication channels
open. Be fair and honest in your appreciation of jobs well done!

PERIODICALLY EVALUATE EACH PERSON'S PERFORMANCE

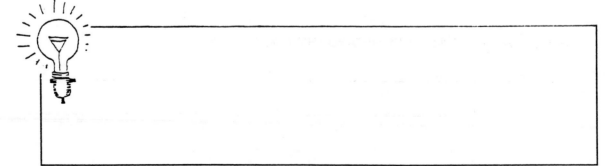

Employee Evaluation

NAME: _____ DATE: _____

RATING PERIOD: _____ TO _____

(1) Unacceptable, (2) Below Satisfactory, (3) Satisfactory, (4) Above Satisfactory, (5) Excellent

GENERAL INFORMATION	Employee	Supervisor
1. QUALITY AND QUANTITY OF WORK	1 2 3 4 5	1 2 3 4 5
2. INITIATIVE	1 2 3 4 5	1 2 3 4 5
3. RELIABILITY	1 2 3 4 5	1 2 3 4 5
4. COMMUNICATION SKILLS	1 2 3 4 5	1 2 3 4 5
5. PROBLEM-SOLVING ABILITY	1 2 3 4 5	1 2 3 4 5
6. SUPERVISION REQUIRED	1 2 3 4 5	1 2 3 4 5
7. ORGANIZATION	1 2 3 4 5	1 2 3 4 5
8. PLANNING & TIME MANAGEMENT	1 2 3 4 5	1 2 3 4 5
9. FOLLOW-THROUGH ABILITY	1 2 3 4 5	1 2 3 4 5
10. DESIRE TO IMPROVE & GROW	1 2 3 4 5	1 2 3 4 5
11. POSITIVE ATTITUDE	1 2 3 4 5	1 2 3 4 5
12. WORK AS A TEAM PLAYER	1 2 3 4 5	1 2 3 4 5
SPECIFIC RESPONSIBILITIES		
1. SALES & CUSTOMER TREATMENT	1 2 3 4 5	1 2 3 4 5
2. ORDERING & INVENTORY	1 2 3 4 5	1 2 3 4 5
3. TECHNICAL ABILITY	1 2 3 4 5	1 2 3 4 5
4. SAFETY PROCEDURES	1 2 3 4 5	1 2 3 4 5
5. CLEAN-UP & MAINTENANCE	1 2 3 4 5	1 2 3 4 5
6. OTHER ASPECTS OF JOB DESCRIPTION	1 2 3 4 5	1 2 3 4 5
OVERALL EVALUATION	1 2 3 4 5	1 2 3 4 5

Assertive Communication

This is the confident putting forward of yourself and your opinions. It is the direct, honest, appropriate expression of your thoughts, feelings, needs or rights without undue anxiety.

ASSERTIVE BEHAVIOR IS...

DIRECT
Behavior is unswerving. Message is clear and non-manipulative. Don't beat around the bush.

HONEST
Behavior is congruent. All signals match — words, gestures and feelings all saying the same thing.

APPROPRIATE
Behavior takes into account the rights and feelings of others as well as your own. The time and place are right.

INTERACTIVE
Takes in what others say or feel without reacting in ways that deny them the right to their thoughts or feelings. This takes conscientious effort.

Adapted from: *Assertiveness for Managers* by Diana Cawood (Self-Counsel Press, 1985)

Assertiveness supports team building. It keeps communication flowing with an open dialogue that moves in both directions. It builds mutual respect and strengthens self-esteem, which effects the person's creativity and involvement.

ALONG WITH INSTRUCTIONS, GIVE COMPLIMENTS AND ENCOURAGEMENT!

Make sure your workers are kept busy and know their responsibilities. Remember, your business is their livelihood and they have a stake in it, too.

Simplified Assertiveness Technique

YOUR THOUGHTS
Without blaming anyone, describe the problem situation as you see it. Stick as closely as possible to objective facts without trying to guess other people's motives or feelings.

YOUR FEELINGS
Use "I" statements in describing your emotional reaction to the problem or situation. You are angry, sad, hurt or disappointed and no one else is responsible for your feelings. You are trying to solve a problem, not blame or prove someone else wrong.

YOUR WANTS
Be specific. If a change in an employee's behavior is called for, clearly state what is expected, referring to job descriptions or company personnel policies as appropriate.

WORDS ACCOUNT FOR LESS THAN 10% OF THE TOTAL MESSAGE.
The spoken message and the unspoken one must be congruent. It's difficult to disguise nonverbal communication. When the verbal and nonverbal conflict, the listener "hears" the nonverbal.

MIXED MESSAGES CONFUSE EVERYONE!

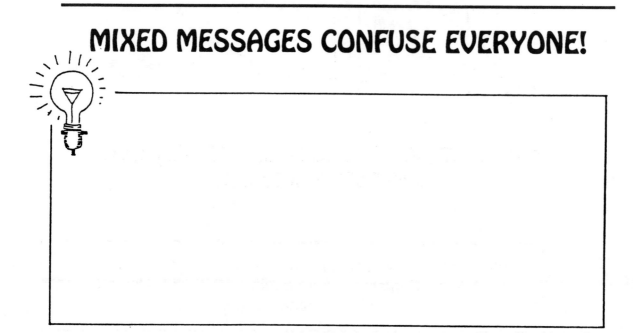

The Legal End

Businesses with part- or full-time employees are required to withhold, deposit and pay taxes to the government. The I.R.S. puts out two publications which explain these taxes and the system for paying them: Publication 15, "Circular E" and Publication 539, "Withholding Taxes and Reporting Requirements."

Simply put, the regulations governing employees stipulate that you must: (1) pay minimum wage or better; (2) insure people in case they get hurt (workmans' compensation); (3) protect them from severe hardship should they be laid off (unemployment compensation); (4) contribute to Social Security; (5) withhold a part of their check for federal and state taxes; and (6) check special restrictions on hiring persons 18 years old or under.

You can eliminate many of the hassles of employee paperwork by starting off with a good payroll reporting system. Get your accountant's advice.

WHO PAYS WHAT?	You	Employee
Wages	All	
Withholding taxes (Fed. & State)	(You do the paperwork)	All
Social Security	Half	Half
Workmens' Comp.	All	
Unemployment Comp.	All	

I LIKE YOU!

ADD AT LEAST 10–15% TO THE BASE SALARY TO COVER THESE COSTS.

Terminations

Because you may have to fire or lay people off, we want to give you moral support. It's never an easy task but it's always better to muster your courage and stand up to a bad situation than to allow it to go on for too long. If someone is not doing his/her job to your satisfaction, and you've done everything possible to get him/her on the right track, you have no choice but to terminate that employee.

Be sure to speak in private. Explain the situation and the reasons for the layoff or dismissal as best you can. Try to avoid any type of argument or confrontation; this does little more than confuse matters and create bad feelings. Be sensitive and diplomatic. Try to part as friends!

Hiring people is a big responsibility. Plan carefully and don't rush into it. Once you have people on board, encourage them to take responsibility and think for themselves. Take a personal interest in their work and be fair in your dealings. Remember, their livelihood depends on you, and you need their cooperation and loyalty to move your business forward.

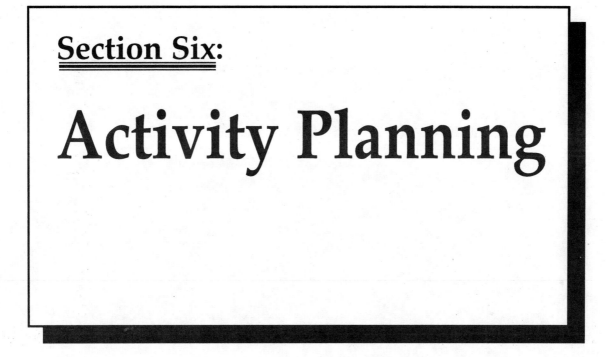

Section Six:

Activity Planning

PLANNING HELPS AVOID CONFUSION!

We're walking a tightrope! On the one hand, we don't want to scare you away by presenting a planning process which is too elaborate. On the other hand, we want to give you all the things you need to facilitate your task.

Each person approaches planning in a different way. There is no "right way" or "wrong way." There is only "your way."

The Importance of Planning

Many people are uncomfortable with planning because it seems too tentative and they don't see its value. We speak of "building a business" just as we would speak of "building a house," but would you build a house without a plan?

Most people don't understand that plans are only guidelines which don't have to be perfect. In fact, we do them in pencil so that they can be changed and updated whenever necessary. Think of planning as writing. It helps you get the ideas out of your head and onto paper. Without planning, goals are unclear and unlikely to be achieved.

The process of developing an overall plan requires careful thought. The idea of putting your ideas into writing — of precisely defining goals and objectives — may seem foreign, intimidating or even impossible to you at first. While you're doing it, remember that you're not seeking perfection either in style or content. Anything you do to plan is better than a shot in the dark. Each hour of planning will save you at least four hours later on.

Planning must be done in the beginning, in the middle and even at the end of a business. Every business has a variety of planning needs — overall activity plans, marketing plans, short, medium and long-term plans. Planning is the first part of the management process.

The most difficult part of yearly activity planning is spreading things out so that the plan isn't too overloaded in the first two quarters. You'll need to set priorities. Remember that plans are meant to be changed.

BREAK BIG THINGS DOWN INTO SMALL STEPS

Yearly Activity Planning

It's time to finalize your planning. In the process, remember that larger goals or objectives need to be broken down into specific activities and tasks which are then timeframed (and eventually wind up on Daily Action Lists). This provides direction and relieves you of the burden of carrying too many things in your head.

For example, if you were to prepare your own taxes, you would select a deadline (preferably not too near to April 15th) and make a list of the steps to be taken. Once decided upon, each step would be placed on your daily calendar and, eventually, onto the appropriate "to do" list. In this case, some of the steps might be to: buy a current tax guide, pick up supplemental forms, assemble documentation, do the actual calculations, fill out the form and send it.

A comprehensive example of the Yearly Plan accompanies the worksheets which follow. This is to give you a clearer idea of what you're trying to do. Once you have quarterly activities, it's easier to decide on monthly, weekly and daily tasks using flow charts and Day-Timer style calendars.

HOW DO YOU VIEW PLANNING?

- Is your business too small to need it?

- Does it increase business stability? How?

- Does it help you anticipate conditions?

- Is it valuable even when it's not on target?

- How do you make a plan and use it?

About Setting Goals

GOAL — something you're working toward; an end product.

ACTIVITY — a step toward that goal; how you'll accomplish it.

Setting long-term goals for your business is an opportunity to dream a little. When you develop objectives for achieving these goals, make them:

SPECIFIC

Distinct, manageable pieces of work.

MEASURABLE

Checkpoints to measure progress toward the goal.

ATTAINABLE

Challenging but not too hard to accomplish.

RELEVANT

Fits into the overall business plan.

TIMEFRAMED

Clear deadlines that help establish and reinforce priorities.

Don't fall into the trap of **only** setting production or service goals. Put together something which reflects all of your plans over the course of the coming year. Bookkeeping, marketing and planning itself are all integral parts of a successful business. If you fail to include them, they may not get done.

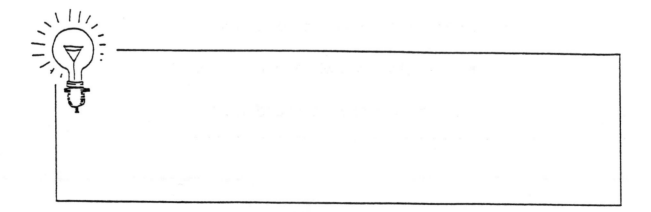

How To Develop the Yearly Plan

(1) MAKE A COMPREHENSIVE LIST OF IDEAS
Starting at the beginning of the book, review the notes you jotted down in idea blocks and elsewhere. Compile a random but complete list of your best ideas.

(2) ANALYZE THE LIST FROM SEVERAL PERSPECTIVES
- The most vital projects for the business' long-term viability.
- Underpinnings (things that strengthen the business base).
- Ease and practicality of undertaking the activity.
- Cost and possible cost/benefit.

(3) ASSIGN PRIORITIES
When possible, give simple, inexpensive (though still impor tant) projects a higher priority than difficult, expensive ones. Use flipcharts and brainstorming techniques to accomplish this if they are helpful.

(4) PUT TOGETHER A PRELIMINARY PLAN
Map it out by categories (Marketing, Finances, Production, etc.) without getting too picky about details at this point.

(5) REVISE IT
Study the flow of activities and the balance between quarters. Too many activities in the first quarter defeats the purpose of the plan. You need to pare things down and really consider priorities to arrive at a balance that is workable.

(6) PREPARE THE FINAL DRAFT
Get input from your business advisors and others you respect before making your final draft.

DO IT ALL IN PENCIL!

Yearly Plan & Activity Chart

GOALS (WHAT WE'RE AFTER)	ACTIVITIES FOR EACH			
	1st QUARTER _____ to _____	✔	2nd QUARTER _____ to _____	✔

TOO MANY THINGS IN THE FIRST THREE MONTHS?

224

Company_____

Period Covered: _____ to _____

3-MONTH PERIOD (HOW WE'LL DO IT!)				EXPECTED OUTCOME
3rd QUARTER ____ to ____	✔	4th QUARTER ____ to ____	✔	

SPACE THINGS OUT BETTER! PLANS ARE MADE TO BE CHANGED!

Yearly Plan & Activity Chart

GOALS (WHAT WE'RE AFTER)	ACTIVITIES FOR EACH 3-			
	1st QUARTER _____ to _____	✔	2nd QUARTER _____ to _____	✔
(1) DEVELOP AN OVERALL MARKETING PLAN	ANALYSIS: Customer profile, competition, targeted market.		CONSIDER marketing mix of prices, products, etc. PLAN overall Marketing strategy.	
(2) ESTABLISH NEW PRODUCT LINE	PREPARATION: Take public speaking course & get presentation together.		CONTACTS: Make list of builders, architects, insurance companies.	
(3) GAIN BETTER CONTROL OF INVENTORY	CONSIDER: Computer system		COMPLETE: Inventory & evaluate suppliers.	
(4) HOLD WEEKLY BUSINESS MEETINGS	COMPLETE: The Business Review		INITIATE Monthly Financial Analysis.	
(5) IMPROVE FINANCIAL SYSTEMS & MONTHLY MANAGEMENT CONTROL	FIND new accountant & review old system. Clean up old bills. ESTABLISH credit policy & get credit cards.		INITIATE use of Cash Flow Projection, analysis & reproject. (3 month experiment).	
(6) INCREASE SALES CAPACITY (PERSONNEL)	CERTIFICATION: John goes to night school!		PURCHASE additional tools & used truck.	
(7) RENOVATE FACILITIES & REORGANIZE PRODUCTION FOR INCREASED SALES	Gather materials to renovate barn. (recycled?)		CONSTRUCT: timbers in main structure & interior framing.	
(8) BECOME CERTIFIED DEALER	CONTACT guild & send for certification.		Study material.	
(9) SET UP PERMANENT RECORDS FOR EACH CUSTOMER	FILE as information comes in.		Study material.	

TOO MANY THINGS IN THE FIRST THREE MONTHS?

COMPANY _____ SMITH & SMITH, INC. _____

PERIOD COVERED _____ Whenever ___ to ___ Whatever _____

MONTH PERIOD (HOW WE'LL DO IT!!)					EXPECTED OUTCOME
3rd QUARTER _____ to _____	✔	4th QUARTER _____ to _____	✔		
INITIATE: promotion & advertising campaign based on our resources.		EVALUATE results & repro-ject plans.			ESTABLISHED IMAGE IN COMMUNITY.
INITIATE: Schedule ap-pointments & contacts for presentations.					NEW PRODUCT INTRO-DUCED TO CONSTRUCTION COMMUNITY.
ESTABLISH ordering pro-cedures, terms and schedule.		CONSOLIDATE parts order-ing for discounts.			BETTER USE OF SPACE, BETTER SERVICE & ADDIT-IONAL MONEY!
DISCUSS incentives & benefits package.		EVALUATE year's work & plan celebration.			EVERYONE "IN TUNE" w/BUSINESS.
LEARN preparation Balance Sheet — P & L. REEVALUATE labor rates & on-site calls.		EVALUATE results & make adjustments. INITIATE other cost cutting strategies.			LOCATE THE MISSING MONEY! FINANCIAL CON-TROL BY END OF YEAR!
John goes on road part-time by self.		HIRE 1 full-time & 1 part-time helper.			TWO SERVICE TEAMS ON THE ROAD!
CONSTRUCT partitions for office space, siding & insulation.		REORGANIZE: Interior space & production flow — make office operative!			READY FOR EXPANDED MARKETING EFFORT!
Take tests.		Get identification cards & number.			SATISFACTION & GREATER RECOGNITION.
REVIEW filing techniques.		INITIATE new procedures.			SMOOTHER RUNNING OFFICE.

NOTE: These examples are taken from various client work-sheets and do not necessarily go together as a compre-hensive plan. We've tried to show you how different people "map out" their ideas. We hope it provides food for thought.

SPACE THINGS BETTER!

Organize Your Ideas for the Month

Using the Yearly Plan, transfer the activities listed for the 1st Quarter onto the Monthly Breakdown chart (inside page 219). Then consider the specific tasks that need to be accomplished to undertake each activity. Spread them out evenly over the entire three-month period.

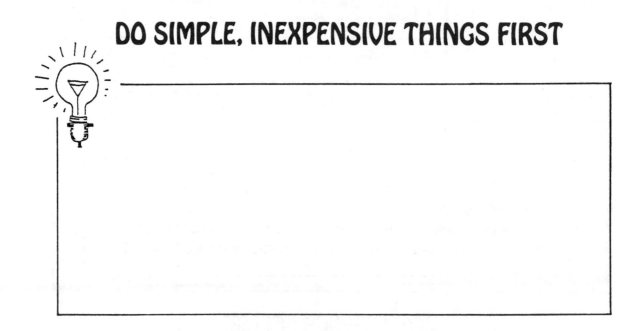

DO SIMPLE, INEXPENSIVE THINGS FIRST

YOU CAN'T BE ALL THINGS TO ALL PEOPLE!

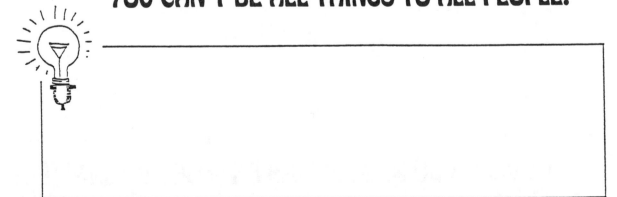

Monthly Breakdown of Activities

ACTIVITIES THIS QUARTER (TAKEN FROM YEARLY PLAN)	MONTH OF:

NOW! IF YOU REALLY WANT TO GET ORGANIZED...

Company: _____

Dates: _____ to _____

SPECIFIC TASKS & PROJECTS EACH MONTH

WHO?	✔	MONTH OF:	WHO?	✔	MONTH OF:	WHO?	✔

TRANSFER IT ALL TO A BIG WALL CALENDAR!!!

Test and Refine Your Ideas

When you set goals, make sure they are achievable. Use other people as a sounding board for your ideas and to help refine your plans. Get the advice of friends, acquaintances, employees, customers, suppliers, bankers, etc. — it's free! Professional assistance, of course, will cost something, but may be worth the investment for the savings in time, energy and money.

BANKERS & ACCOUNTANTS deal with all types of businesses daily. Their technical know-how and experience, especially in financial analysis, can be invaluable. In the section on **Basic Finances**, we are more specific about how they can help out.

OTHER PROFESSIONALS (lawyers, management or marketing consultants, etc.) can assist in their areas of expertise. They can help you anticipate problems and deal more effectively with complex situations. This saves you needless headaches and improves your plan of action.

SUPPLIERS are probably your best sources of production or product-oriented technical assistance. Talk with them regularly. Information about competitors, new regulations and conditions in your industry is usually available for the asking. Suppliers can also provide marketing assistance and hints about financial management.

TRADE ASSOCIATIONS are good sources of contacts and information relevant to your type of business. They help with product promotions, meetings and idea exchanges, group medical plans, training opportunities, etc. Locate your trade association through the *Encyclopedia of Associations* at your local library.

CHAMBERS OF COMMERCE & BUSINESS CLUBS offer opportunities for workshops, seminars and social get-togethers. Through them you can meet other local businesspeople who could be helpful.

FEDERAL & STATE GOVERNMENT agencies sometimes operate as "clearing houses" of information and referrals. Check with the Small Business Administration or your State Development Office. Free business consultations are often available through Small Business Development Centers and SCORE (Service Corps of Retired Executives). Before using these services, however, it's important to know the right questions to ask.

SHOP AROUND FOR THE RIGHT HELP!

Independent Study Helps

LIBRARIES now have a tremendous array of services and are excellent places to look for information. If your library doesn't have exactly what you need, get suggestions about where to search. Through inter-library loans you can find almost any book. A good librarian can be most helpful!

BOOKSTORES sometimes carry a good selection of business- and management-related publications. They are always glad to special-order books if you supply the title, author and publisher. Mail-order book suppliers sometimes specialize in business publications. By requesting catalogues and answering ads in a few business magazines, you'll be on all of the mailing lists in no time!

ADULT EDUCATION is a great opportunity to learn new skills. Check with local high schools and vocational schools about their programs, business-related courses are frequently offered.

Also watch for special talks, seminars and workshops in your area which may be sponsored by local banks, chambers of commerce or associations. Such events are usually inexpensive or free, and you can learn a lot in a short time.

Other Recommended Reading

SmartStart Your (State) Business
State-specific startup series from The Oasis Press®
ISBN: varies state to state

This all-in-one, easy-to-understand guide will help you get started on the right foot. Packed with valuable start-up information, SmartStart Your (State) Business will prepare you to deal with federal, state, and local regulations imposed on small businesses. This concise, friendly, up-to-date sourcebook is an affordable investment that details each critical step of starting your own business — from choosing your business structure that fits your company's needs; to writing a top-notch business plan; to the latest financing options available in your state to handling your business' financial statements.

The Essential Corporation Handbook
by Carl J. Sniffen
ISBN: 1-55571-361-0

A comprehensive reference of the types of small business corporations anywhere in the United States. It explains the legal requirements for maintaining a corporation in good standing. Features sample corporate documents, which are annotated by the author to show what you should look for. Tells how to avoid personal liability as an officer, director, or shareholder.

The Essential Limited Liability Corporation Handbook
by Corporate Agents, Inc.
ISBN: 1-55571-361-0

Tells you everything you need to know about setting up a limited liability company or converting an existing business. Presents difficult financial and legal concepts in simple language and answers the questions most asked be entrepreneurs and small business owners when considering an LLC formation. Provides you with a certificate of formation and a sample operating agreement.

Home Business Made Easy
by David Hanania
ISBN: 1-55571-428-5

An easy-to-follow guide to help you decide if starting a home business is right for you. Takes you on a tour of 153 home business options to start your decision process. Author David Hanania also provides potential business owners on the fiscal aspects of small startups, from financing sources to dealing with the IRS.

Retail in Detail
by Ronald L. Bond
ISBN: 1-55571-371-8

Covers all the steps of planning, opening, and managing a retail store of your own, beginning with an honest assessment of whether you are really suited to running a business. Contains practical information on planning a store opening, from selecting a product line and hiring employees to buying initial inventory and obtaining the required permits, licenses, and tax numbers.

**For more information about The Oasis Press®
and the business titles we carry, call 1-800-228-2275**

Moonlighting
Earn a Second Income at Home
by Jo Friehbieter-Mueller
ISBN: 1-55571-406-4

It is projected that half of the homes in America are expected to house some type of business by the year 2000. Moonlighting takes the idea of starting your own home-based business a step further. It will show you how, in realistic and achievable steps, how you can initially pursue your small business dream part-time, instead of quitting your job and trying your new business idea without a financial safety net. This confidence-building guide will help motivate you by showing you the best steps toward setting your plan in motion.

Which Business?
Help in Selecting
Your New Venture
by Nancy Drescher
ISBN: 1-55571-342-4

A compendium of real business opportunities, not just "hot" new ventures that often have limited earning potential. Which Business? will help you define your skills and interests by exploring your dreams and how you think about business. Lean from profiles of 24 business areas, reviewing how each got their start and problems and successes that they have experienced.

Start Your Business
by The Oasis Press®
ISBN: 1-55571-363-7

An all-in-one business planning guide that highlights major requirements and issues a new business owner needs to know, including startup financing, marketing strategies, creating a business plan, and even environmental laws. Checklists and plans of action ensure that you have all of your bases covered. Also includes state and federal agencies that can provide answers.

Visit PSI Research Online

http://www.psi-research.com

For information about starting and keeping your business up and running be sure to visit The Oasis Press® Web site. It contains useful information for small business entrepreneurs, as well as federal and state specific resources and links. It also contains information for you to contact associations and organizations that can further assist you in meeting your business goals. We also offer a convenient way for you to find information on our complete listing of small business products, as well as convenient ways to order books and software online.

**For more information about The Oasis Press®
and the business titles we carry, call 1-800-228-2275**

A Word About Computers

The world of computers is so fast-paced and exciting that it literally changes every day. Even computer experts have trouble keeping up with the breakthroughs and technological advances.

WILL A COMPUTER HELP?

It depends on the type of business, its stage of development, its capital availability, and your knowledge of computers. Ask yourself . . .

- Do I need it right now?

- Will it improve my business or simplify my life?

- Will it help me do things I couldn't do otherwise?

- Will it pay dividends or directly help me make money?

- Can I dedicate the time needed to get it on line?

- Can I justify the expense?

A computer, no matter how valuable, is not an end-all or an absolute prerequisite for most micro businesses. It won't solve all your problems and it won't manage your business for you.

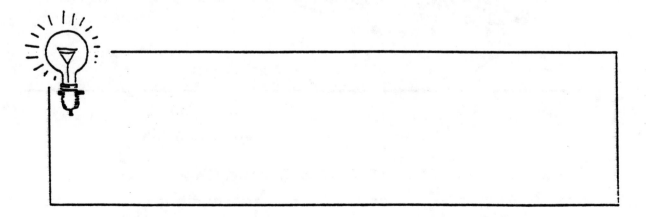

Choosing A Computer

Unless you're knowledgeable about computers, find an impartial business advisor to help you evaluate the pros and cons of getting a computer. Someone who is "impartial" regularly uses computers and isn't biased against them, doesn't have a vested interest in selling you something, and, probably, is paid a consulting fee for his or her services.

You can find such a person by talking with successful business people in your community. Ask about business advisors as well as trustworthy, dependable computer specialists in your area. Also inquire about their computer systems. What do they like or dislike about them? How much time and energy did it take for them to get their systems on line?

Logo used with permission of
Maverick Computer Systems, Farmington, ME

What constitutes a good working computer system is finding a harmonious relationship between the hardware and the software.

ONCE YOU HAVE IT, BACK IT UP!

Computer Do's & Don'ts

DO

...remember that it takes time and patience to learn a computer system and work out the bugs. Factor extra time into your planning.

...think about where you'll have the system serviced **before** you buy it. Depending only on a manufacturer's warranty isn't good enough. Pay the extra to go to a specialist from the start.

...understand manual bookkeeping before doing it on the computer. Even the excellent accounting software now available can't give you all the answers. It may be easier to do some procedures by hand using a one-write system.

DON'T

...purchase a computer system without expert advice, and don't buy software sight unseen. Save time and money by hiring someone to help you get it right the first time.

...listen to your friends. You may not need the biggest, fastest machine. Something less sophisticated and less expensive may be more appropriate.

...get a computer because you want to cut labor costs. In the average small business, computers usually make more work.

...take a computer course at the local high school. The information will probably be out-of-date and, if you don't have a computer at home to practice on, the benefits will be few.

...be afraid to use the computer once you get it. You won't ruin anything through inexperience. Your computer specialist can bail you out of most problems encountered.

Computer Applications

- Computers are particularly good for financial projections and planning. They are especially helpful in managing large numbers of accounts, complicated delivery schedules or several employees on the payroll.

- A computer equipped with software for graphics and desktop publishing can significantly bolster your marketing efforts — designing ads and fliers, managing a mailing list, etc.

- If you run a retail business with a sizeable inventory, check into point-of-sale software. The computer will replace your cash register and keep your inventory up-to-date.

- Certain types of businesses will waste time and seriously compromise their successful operations by trying to operate *without* a computer. For example, a logger who sells trees to wood yards and is always calculating rates and trucking costs would be far less efficient and competitive.

IF IT'S TWO THUMBS UP, GO FOR IT!

Computers are a sign of our times and a trend which can help us take the next giant step forward in our micro enterprises.

A LITTLE EFFORT CAN GO A LONG WAY!

DID YOU DO THE WHOLE THING OR A BIG PART OF IT?
CONGRATULATIONS!

YOU'VE TAKEN A GIANT STEP
TOWARD MANAGING YOUR BUSINESS!

In order to stay on top of things, we suggest that you conduct a comprehensive business review at least once or twice a year. Make overall business appraisals a regular part of your business meetings.

You may find getting through the planning process to be the hardest part since it takes so much time, effort, careful thought and patient juggling. Now that you've done it, use it!

You might begin by jotting down some of your planning ideas (specific tasks and activities) and a few notes to yourself on your shop calendar...just so you don't forget.

Review your Yearly Plan and Activities Chart and your Monthly Breakdown frequently (once a month, at least). Make modifications as they appear necessary. This is our way of working smarter, not harder. We hope it works for you!

Establish a Framework for Excellence With
The Successful Business Library

P.O. Box 3727

Central Point, OR

97502-0032

CALL DIRECT

1-800-228-2275

FAX LINE:

541-476-1479

EMAIL

info@psi-research.com

Fastbreaking changes in technology and the global marketplace continue to create unprecedented opportunities for businesses through the '90s. With these opportunities, however, will also come many new challenges. Today, more than ever, businesses, especially small businesses, need to excel in all areas of operation to complete and succeed in an ever-changing world.

The Successful Business Library takes you through the '90s and beyond, helping you solve the day-to-day problems you face now, and prepares you for the unexpected problems you may be facing next. You receive up-to-date and practical business solutions, which are easy to use and easy to understand. No jargon or theories, just solid, nuts-and-bolts information.

Whether you are an entrepreneur going into business for the first time or an experienced consultant trying to keep up with the latest rules and regulations, The Successful Business Library provides you with the step-by-step guidance, and action-oriented plans you need to succeed in today's world. As an added benefit, PSI Research/The Oasis Press® unconditionally guarantees your satisfaction with the purchase of any book or software program in our catalog.

Our Web site can also assist you in finding your business needs.

The Oasis Press Online
http://www.psi-research.com
Where Business Talks To Business

*W*e not only offer detailed information about every title we publish on our Web site, but walk you through the steps you should consider if you are starting a new business or franchise, plus direct links to associations, state and federal agencies, and resources to keep you up and running. Check our Website anytime for new titles, resources, and the latest news!

From The Leading Publisher of Small Business Information
Books that save you time and money.

Saves costly consultant or staff hours in creating company personnel policies. Provides model policies on topics such as employee safety, leaves of absence, flex time, smoking, substance abuse, sexual harassment, performance improvement, and grievance procedures. For each subject, practical and legal ramifications are explained, and a choice of alternate policies is presented.

Company Policy and Personnel Workbook   ***Pages: 338***
Paperback: $29.95   ***ISBN: 1-55571-365-3***
Binder Edition: $49.95   ***ISBN: 1-55571-354-5***

In direct response to the ever-growing need for up-to-date business information, PSI Research/The Oasis Press® is proud to announce the combination of it most popular book Start Your Business with an easy-to-use, step-by-step software addition. This book and disk package is a perfect combination for any beginning business looking for current information fast... as well as a logical step after reading *SmartStart*!

Start Your Business   ***Pages: 200 + PC Compatible Disk***
Book & Disk Package: $24.95

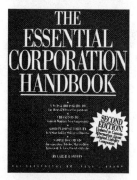

This comprehensive reference of small business corporations in all 50 states plus Washington D.C., explains the legal requirements for maintaining a corporation in good standing. Features many sample corporate documents which are annotated by the author to show what to look for and what to look out for. Tells how to avoid personal liability as an officer, director or shareholder.

The Essential Corporation Handbook   ***Pages: 244***
Paperback: $21.95   ***ISBN: 1-55571-342-4***

This book offers the answers to the many questions a new business owner may have about determining the right site for a new business. Includes tables and checklists to consider before you decide to rent, build, or lease.

Location, Location, Location: How To Select The Best Site For Your Business
Paperback; $19.95   ***ISBN: 1-55571-376-9***

Call toll free to order 1-800-228-2275   PSI Research   P.O. Box 3727   Central Point, Oregon 97502   FAX 541-476-1479

From The Leading Publisher of Small Business Information
Books that save you time and money.

An extensive summary of every imaginable tax break that is still available in today's "reform" tax environment. Deals with the various entities that the owner/manager may choose to operate a business. Identifies a wide assortment of tax deduction, fringe benefits, and tax deferrals. Includes a simplified checklist of recent tax law changes with an emphasis on tax breaks.

Top Tax Saving Ideas for Today's Small Business   *Pages: 320*
Paperback; $16.95   **ISBN: 1-55571-343-2**

Makes understanding the economics of your business simple. Explains the basic accounting principles that relate to any business. Step-by-step instructions for generating accounting statements and interpreting them, spotting errors, and recognizing warning signs. Discusses how creditors view financial statements.

Business Owners' Guide to Accounting and Bookkeeping   *Pages: 150*
Paperback $19.95   **ISBN: 1-55571-156-1**

Essential for the small business operator in search of capital, this helpful, hands-on guide simplifies the loan application process. *The Insider's Guide to Small Business Loans* is an easy-to-follow roadmap designed to help you cut through the red tape and show you how to prepare a successful loan application. Packed with helpful resources such as SBIC directories, SBA offices, microloan lenders, and a complete nationwide listing of certified and preferred lenders - plus more than a dozen invaluable worksheets and forms.

The Insider's Guide to Small Business Loans   *Pages: 230*
Paperback: $19.95   **ISBN: 1-55571-373-4**
Binder Edition: $29.95   **ISBN: 1-55571-378-5**

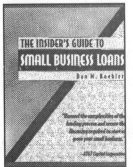

Straightforward advice on shopping for insurance, understanding types of coverage, and comparing proposals and premium rates. Worksheets help you identify and weigh the risks a particular business is likely to face, then helps determine if any of those might be safely self-insured or eliminated. Request for proposal forms helps businesses avoid over-paying for protection.

The Buyer's Guide to Business Insurance   *Pages: 250*
Paperback $19.95   **ISBN: 1-55571-162-6**
Binder Edition: $39.95   **ISBN: 1-55571-310-6**

Call toll free to order 1-800-228-2275 PSI Research P.O. Box 3727 Central Point, Oregon 97502   FAX 541-476-1479

From The Leading Publisher of Small Business Information
Books that save you time and money.

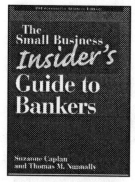

Entrepreneurs can learn how to find the best bank and banker for their business. Seven sections explain the basics: small banks versus large, finding the right loan, creating a perfect proposal, judging a business' worth, assessing loan documents, and restructuring.

The Small Business Insider's Guide to Bankers   **Pages: 176**
Paperback: $18.95   **ISBN: 1-55571-400-5**

Written for the business owner or manager who is not a personnel specialist. Explains what you must know to make your hiring decisions pay off for everyone. Learn more about the Americans With Disabilities Act (ADA), Medical and Family Leave, and more.

People Investment   **Pages: 210**
Paperback $19.95   **ISBN: 1-55571-161-8**
Binder Edition: $39.95   **ISBN: 1-55571-187-1**

Now you can find out what venture capitalists and bankers really want to see before they will fund a company. This book gives you their personal tips and insights. The Abrams Method of Flow-Through Financials breaks down the chore into easy-to-manage steps, so you can end up with a fundable proposal. Windows™ software is also available to accompany the book with all the tools needed to create your own business plan.

ALSO AVAILABLE AS A BOOK & DISK PACKAGE FOR WINDOWS™
Successful Business Plan: Secrets & Strategies   **Pages: 332**
Paperback: $27.95   **ISBN: 1-55571-194-4**
Binder Edition: $49.95   **ISBN: 1-55571-197-9**
Paperback & Disk Package $109.95

Over 200 reproducible forms for all types of business needs: personnel, employment, finance, production flow, operations, sales, marketing, order entry, and general administration. A time-saving, uniform, coordinated way to record and locate important business information.

Complete Book of Business Forms   **Pages: 234**
Paperback $19.95   **ISBN: 1-55571-107-3**

From The Leading Publisher of Small Business Information
Books that save you time and money.

CompControl focuses on reducing the cost of your workers' compensation insurance, not on accident prevention or minimizing claims. This highly regarded book will provide valuable information on payroll audits, rating bureaus, and loss-sensitive points, illustrated with case studies drawn from real businesses of all sizes.

CompControl: Secrets of Reducing Work Comp Costs   ***Pages: 159***
Paperback: $19.95   **ISBN: 1-55571-355-6**
Binder Edition: $39.95   **ISBN: 1-55571-356-4**

Valuable resource for writing and presenting a winning loan proposal. Includes professional tips on how to write the proposal. Presents detailed examples of the four most common types of proposals to secure venture capital and loans; private Placement Circular; Prospectus or Public Offering; Financing Proposal; and Limited Partnership Offering.

Raising Capital: How to Write a Financing Proposal   ***Pages: 230***
Paperback: $19.95   **ISBN: 1-55571-305-X**
Binder Edition: $39.95   **ISBN: 1-55571-306-8**

Prepares a business buyer or seller for negotiations that will achieve win-win results. Shows how to determine the real worth of a business, including intangible assets such as "goodwill." Over 36 checklists and worksheets on topics such as tax impact on buyers and sellers, escrow checklists, cash flow projections, evaluating potential buyers, financing options, and many others.

Secrets of Buying and Selling a Business   ***Pages: 266***
Paperback $24.95   **ISBN: 1-55571-327-0**

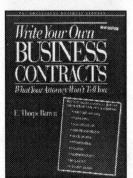

Explains the "do's and don'ts" of contract writing so any person in business can do the preparatory work in drafting contracts before hiring an attorney for final review. Gives a working knowledge of the various types of business agreements, plus tips on how to prepare for the unexpected.

Write Your Own Business Contracts   ***Pages: 337***
Paperback: $24.95   **ISBN: 1-55571-170-7**
Binder Edition: $39.95   **ISBN: 1-55571-196-0**

Call toll free to order 1-800-228-2275 PSI Research P.O. Box 3727 Central Point, Oregon 97502 FAX 541-476-1479